HURRICANE BOY

HURRICANE BOY

LAURA ROACH DRAGON

BOY

PELICAN PUBLISHING COMPANY
GRETNA 2014

To the lost children of Katrina

The word "Pelican" and the depiction of a pelican are trademarks of Pelican Publishing Company, Inc., and are registered in the U.S. Patent and Trademark Office.

Library of Congress Cataloging-in-Publication Data

Dragon, Laura Roach.
Hurricane boy / by Laura Roach Dragon.
  pages cm
Summary: "Twelve-year-old Hollis Williams and his family endure Hurricane Katrina in the Lower Ninth Ward of New Orleans. After the storm, he has to help piece his family together in a drowned city"— Provided by publisher.
  ISBN 978-1-4556-1916-0 (pbk. : alk. paper) — ISBN 978-1-4556-1917-7 (e-book) 1. Hurricane Katrina, 2005—Juvenile fiction. [1. Hurricane Katrina, 2005—Fiction. 2. Survival—Fiction. 3. Family life—Louisiana—Fiction. 4. African Americans—Fiction. 5. New Orleans (La.)—Fiction.] I. Title.
  PZ7.D7823445Hu 2014
  [Fic]—dc23

                                                    2013031747

Printed in the United States of America
Published by Pelican Publishing Company, Inc.
1000 Burmaster Street, Gretna, Louisiana 70053

Contents

Acknowledgments

I'd like to thank the following people for their help and support in writing this book:

Matthew Paine Thacker, grandson of Dr. Lincoln Paine, who gave his opinion after reading the manuscript of this book. His advice was to change the name from "Katrina Kids" to something else because "no self respecting fifth grader is gonna read a book called Katrina Kids."

My many friends at SCBWI and Realms of Fiction, who all have bits and pieces of their suggestions somewhere in these pages: Randy, Rebecca, Teena, David W., Pat, Phina, Carrel, Virginia H., Virginia B., Paul, Alicia, Wendy, Ray, Terri, Sue, Patsy, Damon, Taryn, Hunter, and David B.

Julie Gonzalez, who went above and beyond in reading and critiquing revision after revision of this book. Her suggestions were invaluable.

Cheryl Mathis, whose support and advice I couldn't do without on any of my writing.

Mary Faucheux, who pitched my book to Pelican and found me a second chance.

My wonderful parents, who always believed in my writing.

Gilbert Worthy, my friend and muse, whose ability to help me feel safe at work was memorialized in the character of Mr. Red Beans.

Anderson Cooper, whose support of New Orleans was memorialized in the character of Harry Hathaway.

The late Russell Mancuso, who gave me a colorful description of his time spent in the Superdome after the storm.

Chapter 1

Storm Warning

Hollis Williams scowled as he stumbled on the same hump of buckled sidewalk he'd climbed over almost all eleven years of his life. This time, one of the broken sections tilted under his feet. His angry look snapped into one of wide-eyed surprise, and his arms pinwheeled as he lurched off the chunk into the grass. He kicked the loose slab.

"Guess nothing's going right today, either," he said as he shook a fat drop of sweat off his forehead. "Sleeping away from home's s'posed to be fun. Gee finally lets me go, and the whole thing sucks!"

He rubbed more sweat from his face into the tight black kink on his head, kicked the sidewalk again, and trudged on his way, avoiding other pieces of shattered pavement. Across the street, the noise of a neighbor dragging out her trash can caught his attention.

"Miz Doucet!" After a cursory glance up and down the street, he darted into the road toward her.

The tall, dusky woman positioned the can at the curb, wiped the drips off her face, and grinned. Hollis stood on tiptoes, slid an arm around her shoulders, and whispered in her ear. "Anything left?"

A rich chuckle shook the woman's large belly. "Oh yeah, honey." She poked him in the side. "Think you should?"

"Definitely!" he said, withdrawing his arm so as to better guard his side from her finger.

He pulled four grubby bills from his pocket and held them out toward Miz Doucet. She plucked them from his grasp and, with the crook of a heavy finger, motioned for him to follow her.

"Usual?" she asked as they entered her kitchen.

Hollis nodded, his eyes glued to the refrigerator.

"I'm guessin' you folks know about that storm," said Miz Doucet, swinging open the door to the icebox.

A cold fog swirled into the room, its chill brushing Hollis's neck. "Hear it's a monster." She handed him a small orange pie, and his stomach growled. "There you go, baby."

"Haven't heard anything," said Hollis. "Been over by Darnell Scott's since Friday. They didn't mention it." He raised his eyebrow at Miz Doucet. "There was drama."

Cradling the mini sweet potato pie, he lifted the pastry and took a huge bite. The cold, tangy custard soothed his irritation as it oozed into the corners of his mouth. He rolled both his eyes and his tongue in delight. Miz Doucet chuckled at his expression and shoved a pineapple drink into his grasp.

"Drama, huh. They fightin' again?"

Hollis nodded.

"Hmph! Well, get on home, now. You boys need to help Gee get the house ready. Storm's supposed to hit in the mornin'."

"Fanks, Mif Doufet."

A crumb-coated grin flashed her way, and Hollis disappeared out the door. Another huge chomp finished the pie, and he savored the rich aftertaste of brown sugar and cinnamon all the way back to the sidewalk.

A green Charger with a black nose and clusters of black stars on the hood idled in the driveway next door. Hollis's eyes wandered over the flashy paint job as he wiped his hands on his basketball shorts. Two men leaned into the driver's side window and exchanged money with the car's occupants. One of them straightened and glared at him.

A pang of fear shot through Hollis, but he turned and ambled down the block as though he had no worries. At the next cross street, he eased a look over his shoulder.

The Charger sat where it had before, the men still huddled around it. His heart gave a relieved bounce and, as a seagull streaked past overhead, he raced its shadow down to his street.

Pausing in the shade of an oak allowed him to finish his drink and catch his breath. His house loomed ahead. He noticed a wheelchair sitting on the front porch, and irritation overcame him once more. *What's she doing outside?*

His empty bottle sailed across several feet of lawn into a neighbor's garbage can, and he pumped his fist to celebrate the point before heading to his house.

"Why you out here, Gee?" he called as he jogged up the driveway. "Heat's no good for your sugar." He waved at her right leg, which ended at the knee. "Lost this. Don't want to lose nothing else."

His grandmother pointed a bony, light brown finger. "My sugar? My business! You missed a passel of work today."

"Yeah? Heard there was a hurricane. Boards on the windows yet?"

"Jonas got most of 'em done. He's in the house restin' himself. You can help finish." She scowled. "I'm out here 'cause Leta's busy watchin' those weather idiots make a big deal outta everythin', like they do. Sayin' the same things over and over. 'Gloom, doom, death, and disaster'— over a hurricane! Like we ain't had one of them before!" She fanned herself with her *National Enquirer*. "Came out to let her get her fill."

"Hurricanes are great!" Hollis said, hopping onto the porch. "No school tomorrow." He drifted toward the door.

"Hold on!" Gee snapped her fingers. "I let you spend two whole days out, and you still late gettin' home. You were s'posed to be back afore noon. Havin' too much fun to call?"

Hollis's gloom reappeared, and he jabbed the toe of his shoe into the boards of the porch. "Wasn't too much fun."

"Oh yeah?" Gee flicked her hand toward a spot by her wheelchair. "Park it."

He glanced at her, decided she didn't look too mad, and settled down on the top step. His breath whooshed in surprise. The blazing afternoon sun had left its mark on the step and was now leaving its mark on him. The nylon basketball shorts gave little protection, and he wriggled around seeking a cooler spot. A sharp fingernail peck on his head reminded him to sit still. He did. An angry Gee could cook your butt, too.

Silence lingered. Hollis scraped at the peeling paint on the broken rail that ran along the stairs, and the familiar scent of gardenias surrounded him. Dusting powder, Gee called it. The hotter it got, the more she used. By August, she carried around more dust than a Hoover. Inhaling the flowery smell, he wished she would get on with whatever it was she wanted to say.

"Need to go help Jonas with those boards," he said.

Fingers, gentle this time, plucked at his curls. A smile tugged at the edges of his frown.

"Bad night?" she asked.

Hollis nodded.

"Tell me."

Hollis shrugged. "Friday was okay. But on Saturday, Darnell's folks started fighting, and finally, last night, his dad . . . lit out."

"I see." She brooded a moment. "He back?"

"Didn't come back 'til today." Hollis pulled his knees up under his chin. "I didn't sleep much."

"That why you late? Waitin' to see if he'd come back?"

Hollis nodded.

"Darnell worried?"

"No. He said they'd done this before and his dad'd be back."

"That not good enough for you?"

"No. I told him to stop his dad from leaving."

"And he wouldn't."

"He said he wasn't getting in their fight."

Gee gave a bark of laughter. "Darnell's not so slow as I thought."

"What if his dad didn't come back?"

Gee raised a brow. "Like yours?"

Something gripped Hollis's chest and sent his head spinning. He squeezed his eyes shut as Gee's face blurred. The tears he'd kept away last night threatened to make their appearance.

"Think you could have kept Jonah from leavin' us?" Her voice was tart.

"Maybe," he said, taking deep breaths to clear his dizziness, "if I'd known he was going."

"Oh, yeah." She rubbed the hairs on her chin. "You was in bed when it happened. Well, we didn't know it'd be the last time we'd see him, and I don't see us wakin' up a six-year-old even if we did. Not sure what you coulda done. Man was set on gettin' away."

From y'all. He noticed Gee watching and turned away.

"Jonas ran after Jonah that night. You know that about your brother?"

Hollis turned back, staring. "He did?"

Gee nodded.

"He never said." Hollis's eyes were wide. "What'd Dad do?"

"Nothin' good. He'd been drinking all day, as usual."

Hollis's brows snapped together, and he dropped his forehead onto his knees. A bee buzzed past his ear, and Gee's last words hung in the air. Hollis knew no more would follow until he lifted his head. He jerked his chin up.

Gee had her "I've got all day" look on her face.

"So what happened?" he asked.

"Have to ask your brother."

Hollis scowled. "He won't tell me. When I ask anything about Dad, he shuts up."

Gee brushed her fingers down his face to smooth away his frown. "Your dad causes trouble even when he's not around. Sorry Darnell's troubles made you think about him."

I think about him all the time. But he only said, "Thanks, Gee."

"Go find yourself something to eat. There's ham. That'll make you feel better."

"Not hungry." He grinned. "I also stopped at Miz Doucet's."

Gee snorted. "The 7-11 of the Lower Ninth Ward. Pecan pie?"

"Sweet potato."

"She charges too much. Ah, well. Guess you earned it. All that worryin' and no sleep."

Hollis nodded. He knew she would never understand how he felt about his dad, but talking about it had helped. "Thanks, Gee." He scrambled up and headed for the door.

"Eh, eh!" Gee tapped her cheek.

Hollis backed up, leaned over, and kissed her cheek.
"That's better," she said, and Hollis slipped into the house.

Chapter 2

Weather Idiots

The comfort of air conditioning closed in on him. The outside of his house might have been falling apart, but the inside held everything he needed: two overstuffed couches, thick carpet, and a big TV. It all was faded and threadbare, but it was cozy. And it all worked. At Darnell's house, the stovetop heated up, but they hadn't been able to use the oven in years.

Hollis's backpack hit the floor, and he wandered over to the TV, where his nine-year-old sister Leta and five-year-old brother Algernon crowded close, their eyes fixed on the screen. Peering over Leta's pigtails, Hollis saw a picture of the Gulf of Mexico with a huge swirl of clouds covering the entire region.

"That the storm?" he asked. "Sure is big."

Leta nodded.

"Still coming our way?"

"Yeah," she answered, not taking her eyes off the screen. "Gee needs to keep up. It's already a category five." She turned around with a significant look. "Worse than Betsy. She was only a three."

"Won't matter if Gee watches. She's out there going off about 'weather idiots' again. Anyway, it's not like she can stop it. Is it really hitting tomorrow?"

"I guess. You missed the market."

"Yeah? Who went—not Algie?"

Leta laughed. "No, or we'd be up to our ears in 'nanna sausages.' Jonas drove and I got the hurricane food."

"Poptarts?"

"Yep. And SPAM."

Hollis winced. "No!"

Leta grinned. "No. I know you hate it."

"Crowded?"

"Very."

"What did Jonas do while you got everything?"

"Flirted! With Aisha Chase."

"She's a new one. Figures he wouldn't help when he had you along to do the work."

The front door opened and Gee hollered, "Hollis! I need you." Hollis hurried over and struggled to roll her inside. Once the door was shut behind him, he used the toe of his shoe to lock her wheels in place.

"Leta, turn off that TV. You and Algie have seen enough, and I can't take anymore. Hollis, find your brother and get those boards done."

As Hollis turned to leave the room, Algie climbed up on the couch and started bouncing.

"Why we ain't l-leavin', Gee? They s-sayin' on the TV w-we gotta leave. Where can we g-go?"

Hollis froze, wanting to hear her answer.

Gee's voice lashed out. "Algie! What have I told you about jumpin' on the furniture! Leta! I said turn off that TV!"

Algie dropped to his knees and scrambled to sit with his hands in his lap. Leta fumbled with the controller, and the television went dark.

"We're not leavin' because I'm not spendin' ten or so hours on the road just to turn around and come home again. My back won't take it."

"We didn't go anywhere when Ivan hit last year, did we Gee?" Leta asked. She reached around Algie and hugged him. "And nothing happened."

"Ivan. He missed us. Most of 'em do. Those fools who ran away back then looked real silly when they hit town again, didn't they?"

"I guess," Algie said. "Can I have a snack?"

"No cookies," Gee warned.

Algie disappeared into the kitchen.

"Gee?" Leta asked, watching Algie go. "What if it doesn't miss us?

The TV said this storm is going to be really, really bad, and it might not turn."

"Well, it'll have to. I don't have the money to traipse off to Baton Rouge or Texas like other folks do. No one in the Ninth Ward's gonna leave no matter what those weather idiots say. Most folks on this block don't even own a car."

Algie reappeared from the kitchen with an orange in hand for Leta to peel.

"Now, hush," said Gee. "Leta, you and Algie start gettin' stuff offa the floor in case water comes in. I see you over there, Hollis. How come you ain't hammerin' yet?"

Hollis vanished into the hall. He found Jonas coming down from the attic. A tall, thin boy, Jonas wore his black hair in jaw-length braids. Gee liked to call Jonas names like "Pencil" and "Spaghetti" because of his lankiness.

"Hey, Blues," Jonas said.

Hollis stopped wondering what Jonas had been doing up in the tiny, hot attic. "Told you to stop calling me that. It's stupid."

"Why? You lookin' miserable as always. Blues fits, so Blues it is."

Hollis's talk with Gee came back to him. "You could make me feel better."

"Why would I wanna do that?" Jonas said, laughing.

Hollis didn't answer.

Jonas stopped laughing. "Okay, how? Ya got me curious."

"You could tell me about when Dad left. Gee said you chased him."

Jonas's face darkened. With a wave of his hand, he turned away. "No point bringin' that up. He's gone. Let be." He headed off down the hall.

Hollis watched him go. *Just like I said. Always goes quiet.* Then he remembered why he was in the hall. "Hold up! I'm s'posed to help finish getting the boards on the windows."

"Well, come on! We gotta clear the yard, too. Bikes, toys, lawn chairs."

"Yeah, those chairs are light. They'd fly all over." Hollis sent another curious glance up at the attic door before following Jonas down the hall.

Chapter 3

Anticipation

Dinner was the pizza Gee had been saving for Hollis's upcoming birthday. After a sleepless night at Darnell's house, the work bringing everything in from outside, and the job of nailing the rest of the boards with Jonas, Hollis was ready for bed right after dinner. His eyes drooped as he snuggled his cheek against his pillow. Jonas turned out the light and told Algie that if he farted as much tonight as he did last night, he was locking him out in the storm. Hollis never even heard Algie's reply.

WwhoooeeeeeoOOOOoooooooeeEEEEEOOOOOOooooOOO!
The wind's howls echoed through the small bedroom. Hollis opened his eyes and checked the clock. Midnight. The house shuddered and creaked, as though it were afraid. A sniffling sound caught Hollis's attention. He turned on the light at the side of his bed. It was Algie.

"Why you awake, Algie?"

"I never went to sleep," Algie said. "Is this the h-hurricane, Hollis? I-it gonna kill us? The people on TV said the hurricane is gonna k-kill everyone."

Hollis made a mental note to tell Gee not to let Algie watch any more news reports.

"What?" Jonas rolled over in bed and rubbed one eye. The wall next to his bed rattled. He flinched. "What!"

"All the noise's got Algie scared," Hollis said. "This can't be the hurricane. Too early."

19

A knock at the door made all of them jump. Leta peeked in. "We heard talking. Gee wants to know if y'all are okay."

"Yeah," Jonas said. A loud thud sounded against his wall. "Except for that kinda stuff."

"Y'all come on down to our room. We couldn't sleep. Then we can all play cards."

"Algie might," Jonas said. "He's scared."

"Am not," Algie said.

"Well," Hollis said, "he was scared. Why's it so noisy outside?"

"It's a feeder band," Leta said.

"What's a 'freeder b-band'?" Algie asked, his eyes huge.

"Piece of the hurricane," Leta told him. "Y'know they're round?" Algie nodded.

"Some pieces are way ahead of the storm. That's what this is."

"Is the rest of the hurricane as bad as this?" Algie asked.

"No," Hollis said. "A hurricane is a lot worse—"

"Than a regular rainstorm," Jonas interrupted him. "Won't be as bad, Algie."

"Come with us, Algie," Leta said. "We'll keep you safe."

"I'm not sleepin' with no girls," Algie huffed.

"Okay. Come down if you change your mind."

"Get out, Leta," Hollis said, throwing his pillow at her.

Leta caught it and shut the door. "Thanks," she said through the wood.

"Leta!" Hollis yelled.

She opened the door, threw his pillow back in his face, and slammed the door again. The boys heard thudding footsteps retreating down the hall.

"You think it's g-gonna be all right, Jonas?" Algie asked, his face puckering up again. "I've g-got my shoes on, in c-case we have to run." He pulled one foot from under his blanket, revealing a Spongebob tennis shoe.

"Course it'll be all right," Jonas told him. "Take those shoes off, Algie."

Algie shook his head.

Jonas tried convincing him but soon gave up. Once Algie's mind was made up, no one could ever get him to change it.

"Fine. Keep 'em on if you can stand it. But if there's water everywhere, shoes won't do much good. Now go to sleep or go down with the girls. No scaredy cats in here."

Algie lay down. Before he could ask any more questions, he was asleep.

"He trusts you," Hollis whispered. "And he shouldn't. That hurricane is gonna be way worse than any feeder band."

Putting a finger to his lips, Jonas said, "That's need to know, and he don't need to know." The wall by his bed shook again. "Don't think I'm gonna be able to sleep."

Hollis nodded. "Wish we could see what's going on. The stupid boards are in the way."

"Be glad. Windows probably woulda broke by now."

"I wonder if old man Joseph brought in all those gnomes he's got in his garden. Wouldn't wanna see no gnome flying through the air at me."

"You'd pee your pants. They might be flyin' around out there, but they can't get in here."

"I don't know. Some of them gnomes're heavy. Come right through the wall."

"Attack of the vampire garden gnomes?" Jonas pretended to have fangs.

Hollis rolled his eyes. "Sounds quieter outside. Guess it's over."

"For now. It'll get loud again, closer the storm gets. Time to sleep. You leavin' that light on?"

Hollis shook his head and switched it off. He lay back in bed and watched the fan spin over head.

It took a while, but as Jonas predicted, the noise outside started up again. At three o'clock in the morning, the fan stopped spinning. Hollis tried the light.

"Electric's out," Jonas said.

Hollis jumped. "Thought you were out cold."

"Tried. Too noisy. Sounds bad again."

The bangs were louder and more frequent now.

"World War Three out there," Jonas said. "Got your flashlight?"

Hollis nodded.

By seven o'clock, in spite of the noise and Jonas's vampire-gnome stories, Hollis was finally nodding off. Something solid slammed into the board covering their bedroom window. The two boys bolted up, their mouths open.

"Sounds like the gnomes really are trying to get in," Hollis said. "This it?"

"I'd say so," Jonas said. "Never heard nothin' like this before. Good thing Algie's asleep."

"Can the house take it?"

Jonas glanced at the shaking walls. "I don't know."

Chapter 4

Just Another Day

Click.

Hollis shone his light around the room until it rested on Jonas's face. "I'm gettin' up."

"Yeah," Jonas said, shielding his eyes. "Stop wastin' batteries!"

The door opened and Leta came in with a battery-powered lantern in her hand. Hollis turned the flashlight onto her.

"Hollis! Turn that off!" She looked past him to Jonas. "I knew y'all would be awake. Scary, huh? Gee looks nervous."

"How long d'you think this is gonna last?" Hollis asked.

"The news said the storm should be gone by noon."

The brothers stared at each other, aghast.

"That long?" Hollis asked.

Leta didn't answer. "Gee says get dressed for breakfast. I'm gonna go get it started." She closed the door.

The two boys got out of bed. Hollis shook Algie.

"Wha-at?" Algie mumbled and buried his face in his pillow.

"Come on, we're gonna eat."

"Not hungry," Algie said. "Lemme alone."

Hollis rubbed his little brother's head.

"Let him sleep, I guess." Jonas shook the little boy, too. "We'll be in the den."

Algie nodded but didn't turn over.

Hollis and Jonas scrambled into their clothing, using the flashlight to find what they needed. When they were dressed, they headed down the hall, Jonas carrying the light.

"Dark," Jonas said. "Can't see much."

"Gee's acting like this is a regular day. Breakfast!" Hollis scoffed.

"You not hungry?" Jonas asked. "*I* am. Best to act normal. For Gee, anyway. She was shakin'."

"What?"

"At dinner last night, her hands was shakin'."

"Yeah?"

"Bet she's tryin' to stay calm for us. I'm gonna do that. No point bein' scared—nothin' we can do."

Hollis sighed. "I don't think it'll be that easy for me."

"Try meditatin'. You know, like Chinese people do. Say 'Ohm.'"

"Ohm."

"Not like that. You gotta drag it out. Oooooohhmmmmmm. Over and over. You're supposed to close your eyes, too, but I don't think that's a good idea right now."

"It won't make much difference. It's so dark already. How's this s'posed to help?"

"Makes you calmer. One with the universe or somethin'."

"If I'm one with the universe, can I make it take the storm back?"

"You can't *control* the universe. Just, maybe, understand it."

Hollis ohmmed all the way into the dining area, where Leta had set out cereal and donuts. He didn't feel any calmer, though.

The golden glow of Gee's camp lamp, supplemented by a dozen or so candles, transformed the dining room into a warm, cinnamon-scented place that, for a moment, made Hollis forget the noise outside. Jonas tucked his flashlight into the back of his pants, took his place at the table, and inhaled deeply.

"Mm, those candles smell good enough to eat."

Leta appeared at the door, heaving Gee's chair as the carpet bunched and blocked the rotation of the wheels. Hollis ran to help, and as he pushed, he checked out Gee's hands. Sure enough, when she let go of the chair's wheels, her hands shook like the washer did when it had too many clothes in it.

"Thank you, children," Gee said, the candlelight flickering across her face.

"You're welcome," Leta said as she and Hollis sat down.

"Jonas," said Gee, turning in her chair. "Where's Algie?"

"Still sleepin'."

"Good. All this noise outside'll just make him nervous. Pass the donuts to Hollis, Jonas . . . thank you. And watch those extensions around the candles."

Jonas put a hand up to his braids. "Ah, Gee, I'm fine."

Gee shook her head. "Can't get used to all that hair on you. And why you wearin' your new clothes?"

Jonas looked down at his FUBU shirt and long jean shorts.

"Whole neighborhood'll be in the street checkin' out the damage after the storm. Gotta keep up my rep. Leta, pass the milk." He took the carton she handed him. "Thanks."

Hollis covered his mouth with his hand.

"What?" Jonas asked.

"Since when do you ask for something to get passed? Usually you just stand and grab."

Gee grinned. "We should have more hurricanes. Makes us remember our manners."

"No thanks," Hollis said, glancing over his shoulder at the dark edges of the room. The whistling wind sent something clanking along the outside wall. Turning back to the table, he re-entered their little well of light, and the threat of the storm receded.

Finishing his last spoonful of cereal, Hollis picked up the bowl and drank the sweetened milk. He stood and collected Jonas's and Leta's empty bowls, clattering them in a stack to take to the kitchen. Leta rose as well, picking up the spoons. She snatched the donut box away from Jonas's groping fingers.

"There's only two left, and they're for Alg—"

A tooth-rattling boom cut her off as it shook the house.

Chapter 5

Disaster!

Everyone froze.

"Could a transformer have blown out?" Gee mused, gazing at the ceiling.

Jonas frowned. "That was an awfully loud blast for a transformer."

A faint noise began. The sound was like the hiss and chug of a train hurrying along a track toward them.

"Do transformers sound like that?" Hollis asked.

More loud booms shook the house, but underneath Hollis could hear smaller bangs and crashes, as if the train were running into things on its way to find them.

"What *is* that?" Gee asked, still focused on the ceiling.

"It's getting closer," Leta said, her voice quivering.

The *sizz*ing sound grew louder and became a *huzz*ing sound, which expanded until it was all around them. The noise plucked at Hollis's nerves, and he covered his ears. The sound just got louder.

Suddenly, the house jolted. Hollis staggered. Leta fell to her knees as she screamed and pointed at the front door. Hollis jerked around. Water, spraying like a geyser from underneath the door, was shooting into the room. As he watched, mouth open, eyes wide, the door burst open, and a two-foot-high battering ram of liquid blasted into the house.

"Jonas!" Hollis yelled over the noise of the deluge. "Gee!"

"Get to the attic!" Gee screamed, struggling to turn her wheelchair.

Jonas stood frozen, staring at the water pouring in. Hollis pulled Leta to her feet, and they staggered to help Gee turn her chair. Hollis pushed at the stubborn chair, his head twisting around as he wondered if there was anything else he could grab. Water hissed at him everywhere he turned, curling around his ankles and slowly licking at his knees. He gave up trying to think.

Grunting with effort, he and Leta each pushed at a handle, their toes digging into the soggy carpet, their shoulders flexing. Jonas, out of his paralysis at last, darted past them to the hall. With his knees pumping and his long legs stomping at the torrent, he held the lamp over his head to light their way. Hollis tried to hurry, but the water clutched at his legs, slowing him to a slog.

Jonas reached the attic door and grabbed the cord that opened the trapdoor in the ceiling. Yanking it down, he reached up to jerk the wooden stairs open.

"Get her!" Leta yelled to Jonas. "Put the lantern in the attic and help her up."

Gee sat in her chair as though frozen. Her eyes, wild and unfocused, stared at the water. Although her mouth hung open, she didn't seem to be breathing.

It's like she's already drowned, Hollis thought as he stared at her in horror. Water gurgled at his hips.

Jonas pulled Gee out of her chair into an embrace and backed up the stairs. Leta struggled with Gee's legs. Hollis had just moved to help when they heard a scream.

"Algie!" Leta gasped.

"I'll get him," Hollis yelled.

He clicked on his flashlight and struggled toward the back of the house.

"I'm coming, Algie!" he shouted. "Don't worry!"

He plowed into the hall. A few feet more and he would be in the room. A pang of fear arrowed through him. The chest-deep water would be higher than Algie's head. *I know Algie can swim.*

A new noise reached his ears—scrabbling sounds punctuated by little grunts and groans. *Algie's in trouble!* Hollis surged into the room, his eyes searching for the little boy. He saw him, still in his Spongebob pajamas, standing on the water-covered bed and trying to climb up onto the thin headboard.

"Algie!" he called.

Wading into the room, he tripped on the edge of a dresser that had fallen over and was hidden under the water. He caught himself and stepped onto the dresser to get closer to Algie's bed. Algie wobbled across to the end of the mattress and flung himself at Hollis, grabbing him around the neck and knocking him backwards off the dresser.

"Help!" he screamed as Hollis struggled to keep his footing.

"Algie, stop kicking! And don't hold on so tight—you're chokin' me."

Algie tightened his hold. Hollis turned around and pushed his way out of the room. The water lapped at their necks by the time they reached the attic entrance, where Jonas waited halfway up. He bent down and hauled Algie out of Hollis's grasp and up into the attic. Jonas and Hollis scrambled up the ladder behind him.

His chest heaving, Hollis stared at his dripping family. Everyone was huddled in the center of the attic, the only place where the ceiling was high enough for anyone to stand. The sides of the ceiling slanted downward, roofing nails spiking through the wood. Gee lay flat on the floor next to the others, her wheelchair left behind in the flood.

"Wha-what was that?" Hollis gasped.

"The water," Leta said, sinking down to the floor. "There was so much water." She coughed. Algie joined her and they put their arms around each other.

"Levee broke," Gee croaked, out of her shock at last. "Jonas, bless your strong arms. I never woulda been able to drag my bones up that ladder." Her voice cracked and tears streamed down the sides of her face.

"Not bad for a broom straw, eh Gee?" Jonas knelt to hug her. He helped her sit up and lean against a post.

"You hurt me, Jonas," Algie said, examining a long scrape on his arm.

"Sorry, Algie. Couldn't be helped."

"I got a scratch on my leg," Leta said, rubbing at it.

"I bumped my knee," Hollis said, feeling that he might as well put his two cents into the injury report.

When he leaned over to inspect the red mark, he found himself staggering. He straightened and shook his head to clear it. It wasn't until the floor rocked a second time that he understood. He wasn't dizzy. The house was—

"We're *moving*," Leta gasped.

"I felt it, too," Hollis said, his eyes popping.

"Quiet, everyone!" Gee said.

They all stared in amazement. It happened again. The house pitched like a boat.

"We have to get out of here!" Hollis cried.

"The storm!" Leta wailed. "We can't go out in the storm!"

"I'd rather be out there than in here if the house falls apart," Hollis retorted. "We could get stuck under stuff and drown."

"Water's still comin' up," Gee said. "I'm sittin' in a lake."

Hollis glanced at his feet. Sure enough, the attic floor was covered. "We're gonna drown!" he wailed. "Or be crushed! There's no way out!"

"Jonas!" Gee said. "Get the axe!"

Crouching low to avoid hitting the nails, Jonas scrambled to a corner of the attic. He scooted back on his butt, a short-handled camp axe under his arm.

Hollis stared. *How did an axe get in the attic?* He smacked his forehead. *That's why Jonas was up here yesterday!*

"Where?" Jonas asked Gee.

She pointed to the left, where the ceiling slanted almost to the floor. Jonas crawled to the spot and, lying on his back, chopped at the low hanging boards. Bits of wood flew and the musty smell of old timber filled the room. The work was slow because of the nails, but Jonas still hacked away. Finally, a hole gaped large enough to crawl through.

Jonas sat up, sticking his head through the opening, and ducked back into the attic. "It's not rainin'. I think it's over."

"Thank God," Gee said as Jonas disappeared again through the hole. "Hollis, Leta, help me."

The two children pulled her to the opening and propped her up until Jonas could get hold of her and drag her out. Hollis followed and helped Jonas lay Gee on the roof.

"Don't roll around, Gee," Jonas said with a grin.

"That's enough out of you, Spaghetti," she said, wiping her tears. She stroked his arm. "Blood. You're wounded."

Jonas twisted his arm to see. "Nail. No big."

Leta popped her head out of the hole and scrambled onto the roof, and then Jonas fished out Algie.

"Gee?" Hollis asked.

"What?" she answered, as Leta settled next to her.

"How did Jonas know we'd need an axe?"

"I told him. Years ago, Miz Jackson said people drowned in their attics durin' Betsy, because the water came up over the roofs and they couldn't get out. Jonas puts the axe up here for me when a bad storm is comin'."

Hollis shivered. Miz Jackson was a neighbor. *Have to thank her when I see her.* He gazed around. The choppy gray water had risen so high that the eaves of the house kept disappearing under the waves. The rain had stopped, but black clouds still boiled in the sky.

"Sit down, boys," Gee said.

Everyone sat except Algie, who scrambled on hands and knees toward the edge of the roof. Leta caught his arm and pulled him into her lap.

"Good catch, Leta!" Gee grinned.

"I wanna see," Algie whined, squirming in Leta's lap. "I wanna see the water."

"You can see from here. Anyway, I thought you was scared."

"No, I wasn't! I'm n-never scared!"

"Look," Hollis said, pointing to the house next door. "We're out in the street. Our house *did* move."

"Still movin'," Jonas said, as they felt a quiver beneath them.

"Look at them!" Hollis pointed again.

Across the street, three houses had been pushed into one another.

People sat on the roofs of all three. Hollis waved, and one of the men flapped his hand back.

"Wonder how far we'll float," Jonas said.

"At least the storm is over." Leta sniffled.

Jonas scanned the gray sky with its scudding clouds. "I don't know. It's still early. Think we're in the eye?"

"Maybe," Gee said. "Or Katrina's just takin' a breather."

"What's the 'I'?" Algie asked, patting his chest.

"Middle of the storm," Jonas said. "The quiet part. If we're in the eye, it's only halftime."

"The winds on the eye wall are the *worst*," Leta squeaked. "I don't want to be in the eye."

"The w-worst of the whole hurricane?" Algie asked, his eyes growing rounder. "Is stuff gonna start flyin' around again?"

"Probably," Jonas said. "Good thing you're not scared." He rubbed his hand over Algie's head. "Right?"

Algie nodded, but he glanced around as if expecting something to sail up and hit him.

"Maybe nothin' will get blown up here," Jonas went on.

"Maybe?" Leta asked, her voice squeaking higher. A gentle drizzle made her eyelids flutter.

"Jonas!" Gee said. "Take the axe and cut a two-foot trench along the roof from the hole."

Jonas hacked and chopped, the axe bouncing off the shingles before it bit into the faded fiberglass. The wind picked up, buffeting them.

Not too bad. Hollis's relief was cut short when he saw a wall of rain moving toward them from down the street. He pointed. "Look!"

"Leta! Algie!" Gee shouted over the now-whistling wind. "Get on your stomachs. Take hold of the hole in the roof. Jonas! You lay between me and Algie and help hold us down. Hollis, get over between Algie and Leta and help Leta. Everybody, hang onto the trench!"

No one argued, not even Algie. Everyone did just as she'd asked. Moments later, the storm struck again.

Chapter 6

Stranded

The sharp edges of the shingles dug into Hollis's arms as he clung to the hole. Fearful of something falling on him, he glanced around in the slashing rain. The sound of the wind whooshing off the peak of the roof caught his eye, and, for an instant, he saw tiny tornadoes dancing there.

The wind shifted and drove a torrent of water down the slant into Hollis's face. He ducked his head closer to Leta. A piercing burn across his cheek jarred his clenched eyes open just as Leta's pigtails, with their hard plastic barrettes clipped on the end, whipped toward his face again. He jerked away and laid his sore cheek against Algie's back.

The bangs and crashes returned, but Hollis didn't dare look again to see what was flying around. For a moment he recalled Jonas talking about the gnomes. "They can't get in here," he'd said. *We're outside now. All kinds of things can get to us.*

Leaves and sticks peppered his neck and arms and clung to his skin. A small plastic bottle and other trash skipped across the roof and bounced onto him. Every so often, pelting flecks of debris found an exposed bit of skin. They stung as badly as the time Darnell sneezed while pulling the trigger of the BB gun he'd gotten for his birthday and shot Hollis in the leg. Hollis struggled to see his arms and discovered them peppered with acorns from a neighboring oak.

A long, slow hour crawled past before the screaming wind and brutal rain lessened. The bombardment of the elements finally over, Hollis let go of the hole and sat up, examining the deep ridges the shingles had left in his arms. Jonas uncurled and helped Leta and Algie wobble into sitting positions, too.

"Everyone all right?" Gee croaked.

They nodded. Rising to his knees and then to his feet, Jonas staggered over the peak of the roof and out of sight.

"Where you going, Jonas?" Hollis called out.

"Pee."

"Oh. Me too. Algie?"

"Yeah!" Algie grabbed Hollis's hand and disappeared over the peak as well. Leta waited until they came back.

"Need to pee, Gee?" Jonas asked as Leta trudged off. He and Hollis helped Gee roll over onto her back.

"Actually," said Gee with a wry grin, "my bladder got taken care of half an hour ago. Right about the time *that* hit the roof." She waved at a huge, dead branch that had crashed next to her.

"I'm hungry," Algie whined, as Hollis sat him next to Gee. "Y'all got to eat. I didn't."

"Nothin' to give you now, boy," Gee said. "Left it all down below."

Algie's whine intensified as Leta reappeared. "It's not fair! I want my breakfast!"

Leta took Algie into her lap and sat rocking and whispering to him. Hollis felt at a loss, unsure what to do.

"I'm beat," he said, sinking down onto the shingles. "That wind was blowin' so *hard.*"

Leta piped up. "If it was still a Cat Four, it was probably blowing 130 to 150 miles an hour." She sighed. "I'm tired too. So's he." She pointed to the boy in her lap.

Jonas and Hollis turned their heads. Silence fell.

"Well tell *me*," Gee snapped. "I'm too tired to sit up and check."

"Algie's out cold. Thank you, Jesus!" Jonas said. "No more whinin' for a while."

"Watch your mouth, Jonas!" Gee's voice lashed out. "Lord's name in vain!"

"Nah, Gee! I *mean* it. I was prayin'. Algie could break glass with that whine. And Leta! Miss Know-It-All. How can you see this mess and talk about *wind speeds?*" He shook his head.

"Hollis started it," Leta said, a hurt expression on her face.

"That's okay, Leta," Gee said. "Stuff you know? I'm proud to hear it."

"Thanks, Gee," Leta said, laying Algie down on the roof, where he rolled over and stuck his thumb in his mouth.

Hollis lay back, flopped over onto his stomach, and dropped off to sleep.

Hollis lay on a hot, hard sidewalk. All around him kids played and laughed. His eyes fluttered open, and the sidewalk tilted to a slant and became the quiet roof.

Blinking, he peeled his sticky arms off the shingles and sat up. Algie and Leta slept next to Gee, who lay on her back, a loud buzzing snore blaring from her open mouth. Nearby, Jonas caught his eye and put a finger to his lips. Hollis nodded. He didn't want to wake Algie, either.

He turned his attention outward. The rain had stopped, but clouds still hung overhead. Except for the rooftops, treetops, and light poles, everything lay under dark water.

Hollis saw their neighbors, Mr. and Mrs. Joseph and their eight-year-old son, James, up on their roof. He waved to them, and Mr. Joseph waved back.

"Y'all ok?" Mr. Joseph called.

Jonas waved his arms.

"Ain't this some jacked-up mess?" Mr. Joseph went on, sounding disgusted.

Jonas waved again.

Neighbors sat or paced on roofs as far as Hollis could see. Every so often, he saw an empty roof jutting up from the water. Hollis figured no one in the neighborhood had evacuated. *Hope those folks are okay.*

"What time is it?" he whispered to Jonas, who checked his watch.

"Three," he said.

"What do we do now?"

Jonas shrugged. "Wait. Someone'll come."

"How long you think *that*'ll take?"

Jonas glanced around. "Might be a while."

"I'm hungry now," Hollis said. "Whether I had breakfast or not. Wish we had some of Gee's cabbage."

"Yeah! Red beans and rice."

"With lots of sausage," Hollis added and then sighed. "Or just some of that stuff Leta bought yesterday."

Jonas nodded. "Before long, you'll be beggin' for some of that SPAM."

Hollis laughed. "Never!" Anxiety bit at his stomach. "I hope they hurry."

"Yeah."

Three hours later, Hollis lay on his back, watching clouds march across the sky. *I hope Darnell and them got out okay. And everyone else. All my friends and their families, all the kids at school, the football team, the coach. Even the teachers.* He sat up. Jonas lay nearby, lip-syncing to himself. Hollis stifled a smile as he watched his brother scrunch up his face like he was hurting. Karaoke-face, Darnell called it. *I'm glad he's keeping that up in his head. Jonas's singing stinks worse than a sack of farts.*

"Hey, Jonas," he whispered. "Think the schools are gone?"

Jonas's eyes opened wide and he sat up. "Aw, man! Course they are. All this water! What're we gonna do? We *got* to go to school."

"No we don't." Hollis grinned. "Not if we can't."

"Stupid! I'm a senior. Got one year left. I miss a year of school? I get behind. You know how long I been waitin' for senior year? 'Sides, basketball was gonna start soon."

"I never thought of that," Hollis said. "Our books are down there. Can't go to school if you don't have books." He pointed at the water. "Or a school!"

"Gotta find a way. Whatta disastrophy." Jonas clutched his head and rocked.

"Disastrophy," Hollis repeated. "Good one." Jonas loved making up words. "You make that up yourself? Or did Trey or Kamal make it up?"

"Me. Kamal couldn't come up with that to save his life." Jonas brooded and then gave a snort. "What's Leta gonna do with no school?"

"Kill herself." Hollis laughed. "Jonas, *everything* is underwater. Not just school books. Our games, the TV, all our clothes."

Jonas nodded. "Already thought of that. Sucks."

"So many things ruined," Hollis said.

He frowned as a new thought hit. *What about Dad? Is he out here somewhere? Under the water with everything else?* He glanced at his brother. *Jonas takes off when I talk about Dad.* A smile crossed his face. *He can't get away now.*

Chapter 7

Chopper

Hollis peeked at the rest of his sleeping family, took a deep breath, and asked Jonas, "Ever wonder where Dad is?"

Jonas's head snapped around like a tether ball on its last turn around a pole. Hollis smothered a laugh.

"Not bad enough up here, Blues? You gotta make it worse?"

"I'm curious. You're not? He still in New Orleans? Up on a roof?" He gulped. "Or under one?"

"Don't care." Jonas's jaw hardened.

Anger flared in Hollis. "I'm worried about him."

"Don't be," Jonas snapped. "He ain't worried about us."

"How do you know?"

Jonas didn't respond.

"What happened?" Hollis's voice grew exasperated. "Gee said something happened. What was it?"

Jonas glared at him for a moment, but then his eyes fell. "He knocked me down."

Hollis couldn't hear the mumbled words. "What?"

In a louder voice, Jonas repeated, "Said he was goin'. I went to stop him. And he knocked me down and left anyway."

Hollis stared at his brother. In a small voice, he asked, "Did he mean to?"

Jonas rolled his eyes and said nothing.

"Oh."

Hollis wrapped his arms around his knees and stared out at his inundated neighborhood. The two boys sat in silence, Hollis listening to the sound of the water lapping at the eaves. It made him think of secrets.

"Sounds like whispering," he said to Jonas.

"What does?"

"The water." He shivered and turned to Jonas again. "You remember much about him?"

Jonas scowled. "You gonna keep at me about this?"

Hollis nodded. "You had him longer than any of us. Who else I'm gonna ask? Not Gee. She hates him."

Jonas rubbed the toe of his trainer with his thumb, something he did when he got upset. The rubber pooched, and he peeled off a long strip.

Hollis watched, frowning. "You're gonna ruin them," he said.

Jonas took his hand away and stared into the water. "You were lucky," he said at last. "Dad was a waste. Never came home except to eat or take money from Mama."

"He worked, didn't he?"

"He worked—and gambled and drank and did drugs. That took most of the money he made. A lot of the money *she* made, too."

"Oh." The beginning of a worry nibbled at Hollis. "He ever do anything or say anything that seemed, y'know, good?"

Jonas frowned. "Used to say 'work hard.' But then he'd say 'play hard,' so I don't know. His playin' got us in a lot of trouble."

Hollis waited. "There has to be something. No one's all bad."

Jonas's forehead wrinkled. "There was a while when I was gettin' in trouble at school. Fights. With kids. Teachers, too. He said, 'Don't let everyone know how you feel. Keep that stuff to yourself.'"

Hollis nodded. "That sounds good."

"Yeah," Jonas said. "But then he told me to never walk straight up to a man. 'Good way to get bashed,' he said. 'Sometimes you have to come at him from the side, or even the back, to take care of business.'"

Hollis winced.

"Man was trouble, I tell ya," Jonas burst out, smacking the roof with his hand. "Haven't thought about him for a long time. What I mostly remember is, except for his job, he never did anythin'. Y'know, around the house. He was never around when we needed him. And he lied all the time."

"Did he steal?" Hollis asked in a small voice. "I hate people who steal."

Jonas shrugged. "Probably. I don't know. He left when Mama found out she was dyin' of cancer. I think that's worse than stealin'."

"Maybe he couldn't handle her dying."

Jonas rubbed his shoe again and skinned off another long strip of rubber. "He just didn't want us around his neck. Sick wife—*dyin'* wife—and four kids on top of him when she's gone? He leaves us with Gee and he's free."

"You think it was *us*?" Hollis felt stunned. "I asked Gee if it was us that made Dad leave, and she said no."

Jonas frowned. "What then?"

"Maybe she drove him off."

"Gee?" Jonas asked. "You're kiddin' me."

Hollis shook his head. "You know how it was. Gee was so bossy when Mama was sick. Everything had to be *her* way. I think he got tired of it."

"Gee was worried. She needed help and he wouldn't give any. What about *him,* Hollis?"

"Whaddaya mean?"

"What about he was a loser who couldn't handle responsibility?"

Hollis glared. "Gee says that. I've heard her."

"Don't matter who said it if it's true."

"There has to be more."

"Why? 'Cause *you* want it that way? Sounds like you blame Mama for bein' sick."

Hollis felt the blood rush into his face. "That's not fair—I miss Mama somethin' awful. But she's gone. What if something happens to Gee? Where would we go? Foster care?" He shuddered. "Got no other family but Dad and, well, Grammy Williams." He and Jonas both rolled their eyes. "And she won't take us, and we don't want her anyway."

"Well, Dad don't want us either."

Hollis scowled. "Dad's a part of us, and I want to know him."

"Grammy Williams is part of us."

Hollis grimaced. "Yeah, but we already know everything we need to know about her."

Jonas frowned. "I'll be eighteen next summer. I can take over then. It'd be hard, though. As for that *man*, you have to wait until you're eighteen yourself, 'cause Gee's never gonna let you look for him before then. In fact, you'd better just wait until Gee dies, or she might never forgive you. She's sure never forgiven him."

Hollis opened his mouth to reply, but Jonas put up his hand. "Listen!" he said as he scooted over to touch Gee's arm, awakening her.

Hollis strained his ears and caught the faint *whup-whup* of a helicopter. Hope flared inside him. *Finally! Help's coming!*

The sound grew stronger, and all over the neighborhood, people scrambled to their feet and cheered. Hollis and Jonas leaped up as well and kept hopping, waving their arms and shouting, "Over here! Over here!"

"Boys!" Gee's voice grated. She cleared her throat. "Stop that bouncin' and sit. You'll fall, and we don't need that."

The two boys stopped jumping but kept waving. The helicopter flew past them in a steady line, neither slowing nor turning. It grew smaller and smaller in the sky, its sound fading away. Hollis felt his heart sink. His hands dropped to his sides.

"What are they doin'?" Jonas asked, his hands on his hips.

"Seems like they leavin'," Gee said. "And now Algie's awake."

Leta and Algie were blinking and stirring. Leta sat up, but, to everyone's relief, Algie turned onto his side and went back to sleep.

Hollis scuffed his shoe against the shingles. "Maybe they'll be back soon," he said.

"Maybe," Gee said. "Y'all miserable up here, I know. No games, no TV. C'mon, Noodle, help me, will you? Need to stretch my back."

Jonas climbed over Hollis and helped Gee sit up. He squatted behind her, holding her up.

She took a long, slow look around. "Couldn't see much before. My, my. We're in a pickle, no mistake. Don't let that helicopter leavin' worry you, Hollis. They flyin' around to see what's what. Got a lot of people to pick up, and they can't fit everyone in that one helicopter, now can they?"

"Maybe they want to see where the people are to send boats," Jonas said, rubbing his forehead. "I mean," he said, nodding at the neighborhood, "where's that thing gonna land?"

"Okay, baby," Gee said and patted Jonas's hand. "Lay me out. I've stretched enough."

"Baby!" Jonas laughed. "You're slippin', Gee. Haven't called me 'baby' in years."

Gee smiled. "You'll always be my baby, Jonas. Each and every one of you. Gifts from my most wonderful baby—your Mama, God rest her." She groaned a bit as he eased her down. "Thank the Lord the sun's not out. There's no shade, and all this water's gonna make a whale of a stink. Smells like sewer and motor oil. Nasty! Listen. If I go back to sleep and Noah shows up with the ark or a couple a gallons of water we can drink, wake me up, you hear?"

The day went on. No boats motored past, but several more helicopters flew by. Each time, fewer people jumped up to wave. Eventually, everyone just watched as the big machines roared by. One or two slowed, hovering over the houses for a moment before flying away again.

"Maybe they're counting us," Hollis said. "And they'll bring a really *big* boat or a whole *fleet* to get us out."

Jonas nodded. "Maybe. Weird to think of boats drivin' up and down the street like cars."

"Hey!" The faint call came from a house across the street.

Jonas waved to acknowledge them.

"Y'all got an axe?" the man yelled.

Jonas held the axe up over his head.

"Can you swim?"

Jonas waved again.

"We got people on the next street stuck in their attic. Our axe fell in the water, so we can't help them. Can you?"

Jonas turned to Gee. "Can I?"

"No, indeed," she said in surprised irritation. "Don't want you in that water. Dangerous. 'Sides, I need you here."

"But—" Jonas began.

"No!"

Jonas sighed and made a "wave off" motion with his arms.

"They got babies," the man persisted.

"Babies, Gee," Jonas said.

"I heard him," she barked, glaring at him. "What did I just say? You're *my* baby! I say *no!*"

"Sorry," Jonas yelled to the neighbor, and he glanced at the sleeping Algie.

The man waved to let him know he'd heard.

"They'll find someone," Gee said. "All these folks on their roofs. One of *them* can go help."

Jonas didn't say anything, but Hollis saw his jaw tighten.

"Listen, Jonas," Gee rasped. "It's gonna get dark soon. There's no light but the lantern, and it's gonna be blacker than my winter coat. You won't be able to see your hand in front of your face. No time to be swimmin' around."

Afternoon turned to evening, and evening darkened into night.

Hollis said to Jonas, "You gotta admit, you'd a' been in trouble. No way anyone could swim in this dark and find anything."

Jonas glared at him. "I'm tired," he said. "I didn't sleep this afternoon." He lay down on the roof, positioned his arm over Algie, and drifted off to sleep.

Hollis sat up for a while longer, thinking that he didn't want to wait seven years to find his father.

Chapter 8

Hero

The pearl-gray light of dawn streaked the sky as Hollis eased himself into the dark water, the axe stuck down the right leg of his basketball shorts. He'd come up with his plan the night before. Get up before anyone else, sneak the axe from Jonas, and swim out and save the trapped family. It would be easy—he was an excellent swimmer. The water was warmer than he'd expected, and now that he was in it, he could see that there was more junk in his way than he thought. But he remained confident, driven by his visions of heroism from the night before. Once again, he saw an image of the surprised look on Gee's face. She'd be mad at first—he knew that—but she'd get over it, and then she'd see. He was a hero. He was grown. Again he saw the pride in her eyes when he was given a medal. (There would surely be a medal.) Then, she would tell him that he could find his father. "Anythin' you want, Hollis. Anythin' you want," she'd say. The smile he'd gone to sleep with last night reappeared on his face.

Hollis pushed away from the house and kicked toward the street. The axe hampered him, slowing his ability to raise his right leg. He adjusted the handle back, but it kept wagging forward and getting in his way. His clothing also felt odd in the water, especially his shoes. Floating back to the roof, he took them off and laid them on the shingles.

The breast stroke seemed the ideal choice, because his hands could clear boards and bits of debris out of his way, and he could keep his face out of the disgusting liquid. A thick tuft of twigs refused to budge. His fingers followed them down, and they turned into branches and then into a ten-foot silver maple, standing where it always had but now hidden beneath the water.

The deluge had pounded into houses, cars, and gardens, stripping pieces of them away, lifting the debris, and tumbling it along to bash and scour away even more. The trees had acted like nets, catching the flotsam in their branches and causing even more of a roadblock for Hollis. He tried to clear a path by pushing aside the laden branches until he grabbed a block of wood caught in some twigs and just missed spiking himself on the nails sticking out from underneath.

Pitching the wood out of his way, he paused, treading water, and closed his eyes to better picture the neighborhood he'd lived in all his life. His eyes open again, he executed a quick side stroke, which took him past where he recalled the tree being, and paddled forward again with slow, careful movements.

The greenish-brown gumbo burbled around his body, trash bobbed everywhere, and a colorful chemical glaze floated on the surface. *Gee was right. Stinks. Hadn't noticed it before. Sewer water and motor oil. Makes sense—bet there's a lotta cars under here.*

A half-submerged Rubbermaid bowl with the price sticker still on it, a toothbrush, and a small contingency of green plastic army men told Hollis that houses closer to the levee might not have survived the inundation. A stiff and staring squirrel revealed that houses weren't all that had suffered.

Reaching the halfway point made him feel more confident. Then something new floated by. As the thing drifted past, one word formed in Hollis's brain, and his heart gave a sickening jerk, slamming it into overdrive.

Snake!

He thrashed at the water, trying to use it to push the reptile away, but the snake only rocked back and forth and turned over onto its back.

Oh. Hollis poked at it. *Dead snake.* He looked around. *Wonder how many live ones are in this mess.* He glanced back at his house, half wishing he'd brought Jonas along. He could see no movement on the roof. *I'm almost there. Have to finish.*

The house where the people had called for help was a bit taller than the Williams's house. He reached up with the axe, caught the edge of the roof, and hauled himself high enough to grab onto the eave. Relief overwhelmed him when he heard footsteps scrambling toward him after he called out, "Yo!" A man's head appeared over the eave.

"You need help?" the man asked.

"No. Got an axe. Where are the people you said needed to get out?"

"Came from that way. Six houses down on the next street over. Someone said they heard people inside yellin' for help." He shot a sideways glance at Hollis. "That's kind of a long way. You up for it?"

The smile Hollis sent up wobbled, but he nodded and released his hold on the eave, dropping back down into the water. The axe stowed away again, he propelled himself through the backyard and headed for the next street. As he swam, he tried to picture what he knew of that area. He couldn't remember much. Hollis squared his shoulders in the water. He was committed now.

Fifteen minutes later and two houses from his goal, he ran across another waterlogged tree with debris stuck in its branches. Only this time, the debris wasn't wood with nails sticking out. It was a car.

The car was upside down and jammed tightly in the branches. Three fourths of it lay under the water. Only the nose and the front wheel wells rose out of the muck. Hollis found a back tire with his foot and pressed down on it, trying to determine how firm the tree's hold on the car was. Nothing moved. Not the car, not even the branches.

Nevertheless, Hollis had no intention of climbing over the car or into the tree. He struck out to the left, intending to swim around the entire obstacle, and bumbled into an enormous snarl of wire.

Before he was aware of his danger, he was trapped deep in the clutches of the tangle. Panicked, Hollis jerked and kicked, fighting against the wire, which only tightened its grip. He began to sink. Whatever had been holding the nest of wire up had released it. The mass was dropping, and Hollis, his arms and legs somewhat restrained, was going with it. As the liquid closed over his head, a cold finger of caution cut through the shock, and he stopped fighting the wire and concentrated on finessing the water.

Careful, gentle movements helped get his head above the liquid. He maneuvered his way back to the car in the tree. His feet found the tire he had kicked earlier, and he stood on it. Head and shoulders now out of the water, he rested and checked out the trap ensnaring him.

"Hey, son!" a man's voice boomed in the morning quiet.

Hollis pivoted carefully to the right and saw a man and two kids staring at him from the roof of the nearest house.

"You okay out there?"

"No!" Hollis shouted back in relief. "I'm caught up in some wire. Can you help?"

"Naw. Would if I could, but I can't swim. Anyone I can call for you?"

"You got a phone?" Hollis felt surprised. Gee's cell phone lay under the water.

"I do. Don't work though. Can't get nobody. I meant call like yell. House to house. Where'd you come from?"

Hollis told him as he began extricating his arms from the mass of wire. Now that he could see what he was doing, removing the wire was easy. It would be humiliating to have to get Jonas out to help him at this point.

"I think I'll be okay, though," he said. "Thanks."

The man waved, but he and the two kids continued to watch Hollis as he struggled to get out of the wire.

"Best reality show around," Hollis said to himself and pulled a loop of wire over his head.

Everything went well until he got to his hips, which were far enough under the water that they couldn't be seen. At that point, his attempts to loosen the wire resulted in it feeling tighter. If only he could get higher up. Out of the water, where he could see. His eyes wandered over the way the car sat in the tree.

He placed his foot farther up the chassis of the car. His waist rose out of the water, and he could see the mistake he'd been making in trying to loosen the wire around his body. After a few quick movements with his hands, most of his upper body was free. One more step forward would allow him to complete his escape! He took his step—or tried to. His left foot, under the water, only moved a couple of inches before it yanked to a halt. Hollis's eyes closed in disbelief. The wire was snagged on the car. Forward, back, forward, right, back, left, right, forward, back. No combination of movements with his foot seemed to succeed. Bending over to work under the water hadn't been effective either. Water kept going up his nose and made him feel dizzy. After almost falling over three times, Hollis decided he needed help. He put his hands on his hips and turned his attention to the man and two kids still watching him.

"You ready for that call?" the man asked. "You stuck?"

"Yeah. I'm the next street over. Four houses down and across the street."

Hollis could see the grin on Jonas's face when he first made his appearance on the street. He still hadn't been able to free his foot. He watched Jonas approach, the smirk just getting bigger and bigger with every stroke.

"So what's new, Blues?" Jonas stopped just short of the car, treading water.

"Stuck." Hollis held up some of the wire. "Foot got tangled up."

"Which foot?"

"Left."

"Gimme the axe."

"Why?" He handed the tool to his brother.

"Worse comes to worst, and I'll just cut off your leg." The axe disappeared under the water as Jonas stowed it away.

"Ha, ha," Hollis said.

Jonas swam forward, put both hands on Hollis's left leg, and disappeared under the water. Seconds ticked by while Hollis felt Jonas tugging and working on the wire. He surfaced.

"Gonna have to get higher. You think if I put my feet down, this car's gonna stay in the tree?"

Hollis shrugged. "It hasn't budged, and I've been climbing all over it."

Jonas bit his lip. "I'm not chancin' my weight on it. This car goes, you go too. I tap your leg once, pick up your foot. Twice, put it back down. K?" He submerged.

Hollis followed directions several times, picking up his foot and putting it down at Jonas's urging.

Jonas finally surfaced. "Think I got it." He disappeared again, and Hollis felt the pressure of the wire leave his ankle.

Jonas came up wiping water from his face.

"Okay, gotta get those people out," Hollis said. "You still got the axe, right?"

"Hang on. I wanna see if we'd've been okay." Jonas rose out of the water until he was standing next to Hollis, upright on the car. Nothing happened. "I guess we would have."

"That's good," Hollis said. "Because I'm pretty sure I've still got some wire around my other—"

Just then, the car shuddered and slid out of the tree.

"Around your other what?" Jonas said, panic in his voice.

"Knee!" Hollis yelped.

The car disappeared, and Hollis was yanked under the water, Jonas right behind him. A moment later, both boys surfaced next to each other.

"What happened?" Jonas asked, gasping for air.

"Came loose. I guess you got enough of it off." Hollis scrambled into the tree. "Man! That was too much!"

Jonas jerked his head. "C'mon. We need to get you back to Gee."

"But Jonas, the house is right over there. Let's get the family out first, then go home."

"Nope. I promised Gee I'd bring you right back. Gotta go now."

"But you know how hot it gets in attics . . . "

"You ain't gettin' me in trouble, Hollis. We're goin' back now."

It took much less time swimming back than it had going over. Only a few minutes seemed to have passed before they were able to see Leta and Algie. Both stood in the same position—one hand on a hip, the other shading their eyes—watching for them. Hollis waved. Leta waved back but had to restrain Algie from jumping up and down.

"Race you," Jonas said.

Hollis nodded and struck out to swim across the street. He remembered the obstacles he'd encountered on his original swim and avoided them. He hoped Jonas didn't remember as well as he so that he'd win the race.

Leta waited at the edge of the roof to help him up. She grabbed his hand and said, "Where's Jonas?"

Hollis jerked his hand away and turned around in the water. His brother was nowhere to be seen.

Chapter 9

Rescuers? What Rescuers?

"Guess he went back to help those people," Hollis said to his fuming grandmother, propped up by her elbows. He'd just finished telling her about his ordeal. "He had the axe. I gave it to him while he was getting me unhooked from the car."

"I saw him next to Hollis in the water, but then I had to grab Algie," said Leta. "When I checked again, he wasn't there anymore. I hope *he* doesn't get stuck."

"I'm thirsty!" Algie whined, kicking his legs on the roof. "I wanna go in the water. Hollis an' Jonas both got to go. I wanna go, too."

Leta glanced at Hollis. "He's been sayin' that all morning. He won't stop."

"If he doesn't quit soon," Gee said, "I'm gonna let Hollis go in the water one more time to get his dad's old belt. Gonna need it for Jonas when he gets back, anyway." She lay back on the roof again. "Can't stay in that position long. I *do* miss my chair, I tell you."

The belt was the only thing their dad had left them. No one much appreciated the keepsake, though, and it hadn't been used on them since their dad had gone. Gee didn't believe in spankings. Hollis contemplated her angry face. *At least, not usually.*

"I don't even know where it . . . " Hollis began.

Gee glared at him, and Hollis realized she wasn't serious. Algie sniffled but quieted down.

"Wouldn't mind goin' in for a couple of cans of food and an opener," he joked.

"Talkin' about food only makes it worse, Hollis," Gee said, squinting at him.

Hollis also quieted down.

"That's better," Gee said after a moment. "Now Algie, you can't go in the water. Hollis and Jonas weren't supposed to go in either. It's dangerous an' it stinks more than ever. I'm thinkin' there's a dead animal around here somewhere. But you can go down and look at the water again if you want. You promise to just sit and look?"

Algie nodded.

"And you can't drink it either, Algie," Hollis said. "It's dirty and gross. You'll get sick."

Algie rolled his eyes. "I know *that*."

Leta took his hand and led him to sit at the edge of the roof. "Let's try to guess what all is under the water, Algie. I'm thinking of something that starts with a 'c.'"

"Cars!" Algie yelled.

"Hollis," Gee said, pulling his attention away from the other two. "If he goes in, you go after him."

"Algie swims good."

"You swim better. Besides, this ain't pool water. Keep an eye on him."

"Okay."

"It's good he's got shoes on. How'd you find them in all that water?"

"He slept in them. Just in case, he said. Great, huh? Or else he'd be barefoot. There was no way to find anythin' in there."

Gee nodded but sent him an irritated glance. "Should've known you and Jonas wouldn't listen to me."

Hollis opened his mouth to apologize once again, but Gee interrupted him. "How I could have stopped you, though, I can't imagine. There've been too many things in this mess I should've known."

Hollis waited. "Like what?" he asked at last.

Gee didn't answer. She seemed to be talking to herself. She appeared pale and shaky, the wrinkles on her face deeper than ever.

"Still early," she went on, glancing at the sky. "Jonas ain't been gone *that* long. Needs to show up, though. Needs to show up soon." She rubbed her forehead. "Have to admit, I'm a little proud." She peered up at him. "Of both of you."

The blood rushed to Hollis's face. "I didn't get it done."

"You tried. Gettin' to be grown, makin' decisions on your own like that. Good thing you didn't get hurt, or I'd've killed you."

Hollis smiled, but inside him grew a helpless feeling of lost opportunity. If only he'd been able to finish the job. Might have worked out just the way he'd hoped. *Anything you want, Hollis,* sounded again in his head.

"Nothin' better happen to your brother, either," Gee went on. Her smile faded. "I'll never forgive myself." She shook her head. "My fault we're in this."

Hollis gazed at Gee with amazement. He rarely heard her admit to being wrong.

"Shoulda got out," she said. "I know that now. Shoulda spent money we didn't have, trusted a car that needed work, begged, borrowed, or stolen to get out. Feel like a fool. A blind, stupid fool."

"But your back, Gee," Leta said, walking up with Algie, who sat down and began smacking his feet on the roof. "You'd have been a wreck after hours in the car."

Gee snorted. "These shingles ain't doin' my back much good. And at least in the car I wouldn't have had to deal with this horrible stench! The smell out here is gettin' worse by the hour."

"I stink, too," Algie added.

Gee coughed out a laugh. "I'm sure I do, too. Miss my gardenia powder today, I tell you! Only thing that makes me feel less of a fool is we ain't the only ones up here."

Hollis surveyed the people on the neighboring houses. "You're right about that."

Gee slapped the roof. "Those weather idiots! It's their fault, too!"

Leta rolled her eyes.

"Came to this city after Betsy hit," she continued. "Everybody said Betsy was different. A 'hundred year storm,' they said. 'Won't get another for a century,' they said.

"Then, year after year, we got hurricanes that weather idiots wailed and warned were Betsys. Worse than Betsy. The Big One. We've lived through thirty-eight years of 'Big Ones.' And *none* of them turned out to be all that bad.

"Closed our eyes for us, they did." She closed her eyes. "Got used to the overreaction. And it was luck, that's all. Who woulda thought that?"

"Um," Leta said, "there *was* that one scientist."

"The one they quoted every year on TV? Ivor . . . somethin'?" Gee snorted. "The guy that said New Orleans was a bowl and that the levees were gonna break and the bowl's gonna fill up? That guy?"

"Yeah."

"Well. Who knew a stupid doomsday scientist actually knew what he was talkin' about?" Gee laughed.

Leta and Hollis laughed with her. Algie crawled over to her and sat back, clapping his hands. Suddenly, Gee began to cough and wretch, and the three children exchanged worried glances.

"Gee?" Leta asked. "Do you have your medicine? I know you keep it in your pocket. Did you get out with it?"

Gee didn't answer.

"Gee," Leta repeated.

"I got what I need, Leta," Gee said, waving a hand at her. "Don't worry about me. Worry about Jonas."

Hollis stood up. "Hey!" he called out to the people across the street. "Can you call and see if my brother's still down there? We're worried."

The man waved and disappeared over the peak of his roof to start the message going.

"Maybe that'll hurry him up," Hollis said to Gee.

Algie tugged at Leta's shirt, and she took him back to look at the water. Hollis watched them, wishing he had something to do. His stomach rumbled. Nothing to do but be hungry.

"The water's gone down," Leta said. "It was over the eaves. Now it's about a foot lower. And there's so much stuff in . . . " Leta gasped, putting a hand to her mouth. Getting up, she pulled at Algie's arm, walked him to Gee, and whispered in her ear.

Gee put a hand to her chest. "Jonas?"

Leta shook her head.

"Praise Jesus," Gee said. "Well, now we know what the smell is. You and Algie stay here, Leta."

What's that about? Hollis wondered. He stood up and stretched.

"Hollis," Gee warned. "Don't go over there."

Man, I knew she wouldn't let me see.

"I'm not. I'm going over here, Gee," he said and walked to the hole in the roof. Pretending interest, he glanced inside. What he saw made him excited. Finally! A way he could help!

"Hollis!" Gee called. "Be careful over there, too."

"Gee, the attic's dry. We can get you out of the sun."

"Hm. Maybe. Leta, go help him."

Leta ran over, and she and Hollis climbed down into the attic.

"Whew!" Leta said and then yelled, "It's awful hot in here. I think it's better outside with the breeze."

"See if anythin's down there we can use for shade," Gee called.

A quick search with the lantern through the sweltering attic did yield some prizes. Hollis discovered a stack of dry sheets on a high shelf and a short ladder deep in the back. He brought them to the opening and found Leta with some paint and brushes.

"What's with the paint?" he asked Leta.

"You'll find out. What's with the ladder?"

Hollis grinned. "You'll find out."

Leta shrugged and climbed out on the roof. After handing up their loot, Hollis joined her. They brought one of the sheets over and spread it open. Hollis placed the ladder above Gee's face and draped the sheet over it so that Gee's face and upper body were shaded.

Leta clapped her hands. "A tent pole!"

"That's good," Gee said. "Thank you, Hollis. Helps to have the sun off."

"There's a couple of stools down there if anyone else wants shade," Hollis said, puffing out his chest. "As soon as I saw 'em, I knew how I could use 'em."

A loud *snap,* like pieces of wood being torn apart, erupted from underneath them and sounded through the air. Gee, Hollis, and Leta stared at one another.

"I don't think we'll get those stools, Hollis," Gee said. "Might not be safe down there after all."

Hollis and Leta nodded, wide-eyed.

Chapter 10

Insulin

"Leta, what did *you* find?" Gee asked, covering the pause after the ominous sound.

"Paint!" Leta announced. "We can use it to paint 'help' on the roof!"

Hollis stared. *She's brilliant! We'll definitely get rescued when people see we have a sign!*

Just then, a voice came from across the street. "Your boy got the baby out!" the man hollered. "He's a hero!"

Hollis gritted his teeth but then responded, "He heading back then?"

"Dunno. Jumped back in the water a while ago. He'll show up soon."

"Thanks," Hollis yelled. He turned to Gee.

"Well, I hope he does," Gee said. "Not *help*, Leta, paint *insulin*."

"But Gee," Hollis said, "why would we put your medicine on there?"

"When people see *insulin,* they'll know someone on this roof has diabetes. They'll know someone might be dyin'."

The bottom dropped out of Hollis's stomach. "Are you dyin'?"

Gee snorted. "'Course not. But they don't know that. Might hurry them up if they think I'm worse off than I am."

Hollis smiled in relief. "Great idea! C'mon, Leta! Let's get started!"

"Algie too," Gee added.

"Algie?" Hollis said in disbelief. "Algie can't—"

"Algie'll do fine. Keep him from whinin'. I hope!"

Hollis didn't have an argument for that. He opened the paint.

Early on, Algie discovered that painting letters wasn't as much fun as making polka dots.

"Gee!" Leta said. "Algie's making a mess."

"Long as he doesn't start paintin' himself, Leta, I don't care. He's happy. Just get that sign done."

"Hollis," Leta said a few minutes later, irritation in her voice, "you're making your letter too big. We're not going to have room for the whole word."

"Gee said to make it big," he said, dipping his brush in the paint.

"But it has to fit. Gee! If we make it that big, we'll have room for *insul* but no room for the 'IN.'"

"Put it underneath, Leta. They'll figure it out."

"Yes, ma'am," Leta said, still frowning.

It took an hour to spell out *insulin.* "There," Hollis said at last. "That's not too bad."

"I'm sure it'll get us attention." Gee paused, surveying the fading light. "Hope Jonas gets back before dark."

Hollis and Leta lay on the roof staring up at the night sky. On Monday night, storm clouds had covered the moon and stars. Tonight was clear, and a radiant, star-filled sky with a sliver of moon gave faint light to their surroundings.

"Look at all the stars," Leta said. "The sky's so crowded I can hardly find the Big Dipper. Guess the power being out makes them easier to see."

"Duh," said Hollis.

Leta frowned. "Why you being mean?"

"I'm not being mean," Hollis said. "You're being stupid."

"How am I being stupid?" Leta sat up. "You're being stupid if you can't tell me how I'm being stupid."

"Fine," Hollis said without moving. "You're being stupid because Jonas is missing, Gee is dying, I'm so thirsty I can't even think, we're never getting off this rotten roof, and all you can say is," he mimicked her voice, "'look at the stars.'"

Leta opened her mouth to retort, but another helicopter flew over.

Hollis hadn't heard it coming, because he'd gotten so used to them flying over without a pause. Startled, he watched as this one slowed and turned back toward them. He surged to his feet.

"They're coming back!" he yelled. "They're coming to get us! The sign worked! Gee! It worked!"

The helicopter hovered over them, and a bright light shot down from beneath it. Hollis went crazy. He waved, jogged, and danced with excitement. The light shone for a while longer before shutting off. After that, the helicopter flew away.

"Wait!" Hollis screamed. He turned to his grandmother. "What was that? Why don't they help us? What's the deal?"

"It was a news helicopter," Leta said.

"What?" Hollis glared at her, panting. "What do you mean?"

"I mean you're gonna be on TV. I could see 'Channel Six News' on the side and a guy with a camera hanging out of the door. That's why they had a light. For the camera."

Hollis flopped down on the shingles, feeling like a fool. Disappointment overwhelmed him.

"Hollis," Gee said.

"What?" he grumbled. *Everyone needs to leave me alone.*

"It'll help. When people see it on TV and they see there are stranded children and people who need medicine, more people will come and we'll get out of here. That's why they're doin' this."

Hollis turned. "They couldn't throw us a bottle of water? A sandwich? You know *they* ate."

He lay back on the roof, curled himself around his anger, and tried to go to sleep.

Chapter 11

Oh, Gee

A pair of loud *snaps* heralded a Wednesday with intense blue skies, fluffy clouds, and the white-hot glare of a relentless sun. Hollis opened his eyes and frowned at the re-occurrence of the noise.

Leta bolted awake. "Hollis?"

Algie stirred and interrupted her. "I'm thirsty, Hollis! I wanna drink!"

Hollis stared at the little boy, whose cracked, white-flecked lips stuck together in places. A gray gook had gathered in the corners of his mouth. *Mine are probably like that, too. They feel all gummy.*

"Was that another one of those cracking sounds?" Leta asked.

Hollis nodded. "Two."

"I don't like that," Leta said, rubbing her neck and twisting her back. "I want to know what it is." She turned to check on Gee, who was lying under her tent with her eyes closed. "She doesn't look good."

"She's fine!" Hollis hissed. "Keep your voice down. She's just sleepin'."

Leta turned away.

"Where is everybody, Leta?" Algie asked. "What's takin' so long?"

"I don't know, Algie. I wish people'd get here. Or Jonas."

We're dyin' of thirst and we can't do a thing. If someone doesn't do something soon we'll be dead. I gotta do something—I feel dead already.

"I could swim for help," Hollis said.

"Yeah. Like that worked before."

"You don't know anything, Leta! I got really far the last time." He stared at the water. Truth be told, he really didn't want to go into that mess again.

Leta's face crumpled, and tears ran down her cheeks. Hollis stared at her in surprise.

"You need to stay here!" she said. "You can't leave me with both Algie and Gee to take care of. You can't!"

Hollis felt ashamed. "I was just going for help. I wouldn't leave for good."

Leta wiped her eyes, a sudden expression of hope in them. "Maybe that's where Jonas is? Getting us help. He saved those people, and now he's going to save us."

Hollis sat down on the roof with a thump. Leta was probably right. Jonas was the hero in this family. Why was he even trying? He pulled his knees up to his chest, laid his forehead on them, and retreated into himself. He withdrew so much that he didn't hear the boat putting down Flood Street about twenty minutes later until it was almost to them.

All around, stranded people stirred and called out. Although it reduced its speed as though in response, the boat—a police cruiser— was stopping for no one. Two officers piloted it, but it was already overloaded with other people.

Leta grabbed a light blue pillowcase and waved it as the prow drew parallel with the Josephs' house. The cruiser slowed, and Hollis lifted his head.

"We're only taking sick or injured," the pilot called.

Hollis stood up. "My grandmother's got diabetes. She's really sick."

The man spoke to the other deputy before giving a reply. "Okay. We'll see what we can do."

The three children watched hopefully as the boat angled toward them and stopped with a soft bump against the eaves of the house. An officer climbed out, handing a small bottle of water to each child. The bottles remained unopened as everyone watched the man lean down to awaken Gee. Gee didn't move. Hollis heard Leta give a little moan.

The policeman sat down on the sloping roof and lifted Gee's shoulders into his lap.

"We should try to get some water in her," he said, holding the last bottle.

Leta squatted on one side of Gee, holding onto Algie, and Hollis stood on the other. Everyone nodded.

"How long she been like this?" the man asked.

Leta shook her head, her brow furrowed. "We were letting her sleep. We wanted her to rest."

"We don't know," Hollis said.

The man opened the bottle. "Ordinarily, I wouldn't do this, because it might choke her. But she's in a bad way. We'd have a better chance of moving her for help if she's less dehydrated, so I'm gonna take the risk."

He dribbled water into Gee's mouth, but it drained out again. Hollis bit his lip. Then Gee's throat moved and she swallowed.

Hollis's knees gave way, and he collapsed onto the shingles. Leta hugged Algie and told him Gee would be okay. Hollis saw the policeman glance at her, an uncertain look on his face. But he continued to feed Gee the rest of the water, one tiny dribble at a time.

"I think that's all we should give her right now," he said at last.

Hollis glanced at his hand, remembering he still had a bottle of his own. He opened it and chugged the contents down in several greedy swallows. Wiping his mouth, he noticed Algie wrestling with his bottle cap and motioned him over.

"Thanks," Algie croaked as Hollis handed the bottle back to him.

The other policeman joined the first and helped him pick Gee up and carry her to the boat. The crowd made room, and they laid her on the boat's floor. Beyond swallowing, Gee hadn't moved or spoken.

Hollis's eyes wandered over the small craft, which sat low in the water. So low that, if a wave came along, water would get into the boat. The people had their eyes closed or pained expressions on their faces. Hollis noticed a familiar face amongst the strangers.

"Miz Jackson!" Hollis yelled, waving at the woman who sat leaning against the side of the boat, her eyes closed and blood on her face.

Beside her, a man with blood on his shirt and arm lifted his hand.

"She can't hear you, son," he called, as Leta and Algie joined Hollis at the edge of the roof. "She got a bad bang on the head when our roof caved in, and these fellers gave her somethin' that knocked her out. I'm her husband, Marvin. This your grandma?"

Hollis nodded. "Her name's Gee."

"Aw, yeah," Marvin said. "I've heard Aletha talk about Gee."

The first policeman made his way back to them. His expression was grim.

"I don't like leaving you kids alone, so we're going to go with this load, then get back here fast."

"Thanks, mister," Leta said. "We'll be okay. We got neighbors."

She turned and waved to the Josephs' house. Everyone in the area had their eyes on the Williams' house, wondering if the boat would take them away. Mr. Joseph waved back.

"Watch out for these kids, will you?" the policeman called.

"We'll try," Mr. Joseph yelled. "But it's not like that'll be easy." He gestured at the neighborhood. "Y'all comin' back?"

"We'll try," the policeman yelled.

Mr. Joseph threw his hands up in frustration.

The men prepared to leave.

"Don't you worry, boy," Marvin called out as the boat started. "I'll take care of them both. Gonna go to Baton Rouge. Look for us at a hospital out there."

Hollis nodded. *First Dad, then Mom, then Jonas, now Gee. Everyone is disappearing.*

Chapter 12

A Gift from Above

Late that afternoon, Hollis remembered that he wanted to see what was in the water by the house. Algie was sleeping, and he and Leta sat on the roof, counting birds.

"This is the first day since the storm that I've seen them," Leta whispered.

"There were some yesterday."

"Oh," Leta said, pulling her legs up, bending her knees, and waggling them from side to side. "I kind of wish it would rain and cool us off."

"We don't need any more water."

"I don't think it'd make a difference."

Hollis hesitated. "Leta?"

"Yeah?"

"What did you see in the water over there?"

Leta looked confused.

"You know, yesterday. You took Algie away from the water, and Gee wouldn't let me go look."

"Oh, yeah." Leta frowned and glanced down. "I'm not telling you."

"I'm gonna check it out then."

"Gee said not to."

"You got to see."

"I didn't want to."

"Well, I do." He stood up.

Leta put her hand on his leg. "Hollis, don't. It—it's a person."

Hollis stared down at her, his breath stilled in his throat. "You mean a *dead* person?"

She nodded.

He glanced over to where the mystery lay. "Then I definitely wanna see."

"No, you don't."

Hollis walked toward the edge, as though drawn.

"I'm telling Gee if you don't stop," Leta said, raising her voice.

"Shh! Don't wake up Algie. Gee's gone. We don't know if we'll ever see her again. We're on our own, and I want to see." He walked faster.

"Oh, Hollis," Leta moaned, breaking into tears. "We *will* see Gee again! She's gonna be fine. Jonas too!"

Shame covered Hollis. He turned and trudged back. Leta rocked on the shingles, her face in her hands.

"Sorry," he said.

Leta sniffled. "No, you're right. Everything's different. Go see if you want—it doesn't matter."

Hollis stood still, watching her.

"Really," Leta said.

"Okay." Hollis hurried to the edge before she could change her mind.

All I see is trash: bottles, paper, branches, somebody's shirt and pants . . . His eyes slid over the litter before returning to the items of clothing. Hollis frowned. He stared for a long moment and saw something he would never forget.

A man's bloated face, smudged and blurry, stared up at him, his body riding low in the water with debris surrounding him. He was hard to make out, but now that Hollis knew what he was looking at, he could see the man's stiff, contorted form, the fingers curled and grasping at nothing, the head thrown back as if in pain.

It doesn't seem like a person. Wrenching his eyes away, he plodded back to Leta. She watched him, still sniffling. He sat down next to her again.

"You saw it?"

Hollis nodded.

"It's gross, huh?"

Hollis nodded.

"You okay?"

Hollis nodded.

"Well, what do you think?" she burst out.

Hollis shook his head. He didn't want to tell her what he was thinking. *Where could Dad be?*

"I've never seen *rigor mortis* before," Leta went on in a conversational tone. "It's creepy. I can see why they call dead people 'stiffs.'" She covered her eyes with her hands and shivered.

Hollis glanced at her. "You feeling better, I guess."

She nodded. "I'm glad you saw. Now I can talk about it with someone."

"What's to talk about?" His voice croaked, and he cleared his throat.

"It scared me, because, y'know, at first I thought it was Jonas."

"Jonas didn't have on a Saints jersey."

Leta grimaced. "I didn't notice what it—um, *he*—was wearing. I didn't want to look that close." She paused. "But after I thought about Jonas, I thought about Dad."

Hollis started and gazed at her. "You didn't!"

She put her head down, and Hollis heard a sniffle. After a moment, she lifted her head. "I did. I thought if I told you, then you'd call me stupid again."

"No."

"Good. I don't like to be called stupid, even when I am. It's stupid that I thought of Dad."

"I thought the same thing."

Her jaw dropped. "You're lying!"

He shook his head. "It made me feel sick."

"The man or thinking it was Dad?"

"Thinking it was Dad."

They sat quietly for a moment. Then Hollis asked, "Ever wonder where he is?"

Leta shook her head.

"Why not?"

"Gee says he's not nice. He's never come to see us. We live in the same place we always did, so it's not like he doesn't know where we are."

"You don't want to see him? Get to know him? He's part of us."

"Gee says he'll just make us feel bad."

"So you talked to Gee about Dad." It was not a question. He felt both impressed and annoyed. Until the incident at Darnell's house, Hollis had always been afraid to bring it up. "Did you happen to ask where he is?"

"She said she didn't know."

"I'm gonna find him. I hope he's not dead."

"I hope he's not dead too, but I don't think Gee's gonna let us find him."

Hollis sighed. "I don't either."

Leta sniffed once more and leaned against Hollis. He put his arm around her, feeling closer to her than he ever had before.

Dusk found the three awake but lethargic. Two more news helicopters had passed overhead. When they heard a third, they didn't even glance up. It slowed, as some of the others had, and hovered over the house across the street. A big light shone on the roof, and a man on a cable, followed by a big wire basket, slid down.

Hollis and Leta bolted up in excitement. Two of the people on the roof got into the basket and were raised into the helicopter. The basket came down again, and a third person went up. After the man on the cable got pulled up, the machine proceeded to the Josephs' house and repeated the show.

Hollis watched as Mr. Joseph pointed at the three of them. The man on the cable shook his head. Mr. Joseph talked some more while Mrs. Joseph and James were raised up.

When the basket came down again, Mr. Joseph called out, "They full up, but they comin' back. I told them you was kids. I told them you was alone."

Hollis waved.

Mr. Joseph climbed into the basket, and both he and the man on the cable rose into the night.

"Everybody says they're coming back," Hollis grumbled.

Leta nodded.

The helicopter glided past them and three more houses before it hovered again. A large box came down on a cable. The people on the roof grabbed the box, and the cable slithered up again.

"What's that?" Algie breathed.

Hollis shook his head. "I don't know, but I'll bet it's good."

"I hope we get one," Leta said. "Think Mr. Joseph told them to give us one?"

"Heyyy!" Algie yelled and waved at the chopper. Hollis smiled. Algie appeared to be waving at a float in a Mardi Gras parade.

"Throw me something, mister," Hollis yelled.

Algie and Leta stared at him and then laughed. They put up their arms, invoking the age-old spirit of a New Orleans Mardi Gras. "Hey, mister, throw us something!"

A few other houses received a box until, at last, the helicopter hovered over them and dangled one of the mysterious containers above their heads.

"It feels like Christmas and my birthday all rolled into one," Hollis told Leta.

She cocked her head. "Y'know, Hollis? It *is* your birthday. It's the thirty-first, isn't it?"

Hollis nodded. "I guess it is. I like my present, Leta. Thanks."

Leta giggled, and she and Algie sang "Happy Birthday."

Hollis grinned and watched his birthday present descend, inch by inch, until with a thump, it sat on the roof. His sister released the cable.

"Open it!" she said.

Hollis pounced on the box. "Help me," he huffed, tugging at one of the flaps.

Leta joined him, and they each pulled. Bit by bit, the glue gave way, peeling back to reveal light-brown packages. Hollis pulled them out and dumped them onto the roof. Four six-packs of water lay underneath. Hollis and Leta each grabbed a bottle and handed an open one to Algie. Within minutes, the bottles were emptied. Once Hollis had handed out seconds, everyone's attention turned to the packages.

"What've we got?" Leta crowed. "Food: Meal, Ready-to-Eat! Ooh, jambalaya. Yum!"

"Chili and macaroni," Hollis read. "Algie! This is what soldiers eat."

Hollis tore open his MRE and dug his fingers into the cold macaroni. Meaty tomato sauce and chewy macaroni made him forget how long they'd been on the roof.

"There's a fork," Leta said. "Hey, this silver thing in here heats them up. Anyone want theirs heated?"

No one answered. Leta helped Algie get his spaghetti and meat sauce open, and then she stuffed the rice and fat pieces of sausage into her mouth.

Hollis picked up another brown package. "Beef stew. Gee's favorite. Wish she was here. We got tons of food now. You think they really mean to come back?"

"Doesn't look like it." Leta paused mid-bite. "They'd better." She picked through the items left in her bag. "There's lots of other things. No birthday cake, but there's candy, cheese and crackers, and cookies!"

"Tastes almost as good as the food at Dooky Chase," Hollis said, referring to the family's favorite restaurant. "I might just have another."

"Maybe we can split one. These are awful big."

Hollis got through a second and picked up some packets that had fallen out of one of his dinner bags. "Drink mixes!" he said, laughing. "Cocoa beverage and dairy shake. Anyone want to try one? Algie?"

Algie shook his head. "I like this soldier water."

Dinner finished, each of them lay back, reveling in the luxury of being full.

"I'm so stuffed I could roll off the roof," Hollis said and belched.

Leta didn't answer. She stared out into the night. "I wonder if Jonas and Gee got anything to eat."

Chapter 13

Basket Case

Leta looked up at the sunless sky. "It's too dark for that helicopter to come back tonight."

"I won't have any trouble sleeping," Hollis said, rubbing his belly.

"We should thank God for the food and the help that came for Gee," Leta said.

Hollis scowled. "Don't see why we should thank God while we're still stuck on the roof." He hesitated and glanced upward. *No offense, God, but seems to me that You're taking Your time getting us outta here.*

Leta insisted. "Gee would."

Algie grabbed Leta's hand and held his other out to Hollis. Hollis shrugged and bowed his head while Leta did her thanking.

"What about J-Jonas?" Algie asked. "Maybe we could ask God to bring him back?"

"Can't hurt," Hollis said.

After Leta added a prayer for Jonas, they all settled back to go to sleep.

Hollis laid his cheek on the back of his hand, closed his eyes, and relaxed, but sleep was far away. *Darn Leta.* Jonas drifted into his thoughts, and Hollis couldn't help but wonder what might have happened to him. What if he were dead? What if Gee were dead? Jonas had said that he could take care of them when he was eighteen if something happened to Gee. Now Jonas might be dead, too. Hollis felt even more determined to find their father.

A faint noise broke into his thoughts. It sounded like the *whup, whup, whup* of another helicopter. Hollis dismissed that possibility. The choppers usually stopped after dark.

The sound did not go away. In fact, it grew until it sounded like it was right above Hollis's head. Looking up, the kids saw an orange chopper hovering above them, and they scrambled to their feet and jumped and waved. A blinding spotlight shot down, and a cable lowered a man in a Coast Guard helmet and gray jumpsuit onto their roof. He strode up the slant just as two more loud *snaps* sounded through the night. A powerful shudder ran through the house.

"That noise coming from this house?" the man barked at Hollis.

Hollis jumped. "We've been hearin' it a few days now. The house never shook like that though."

"Those g-guys came back for us, Leta!" Algie crowed.

Leta hugged him. "I know, Algie."

"Is it fun ridin' on that rope like you do?" Algie asked. "I wanna do that."

"Hang on a minute, Algie," Hollis said.

Hollis turned back to the man, who had a frown on his face.

"Name's Gus," the man said. A basket started on its way down to them. "We're gonna do this fast. All three of you in the basket ASAP. Is this house raised?"

Hollis was confused. "We floated some when the water hit us. Is that what you mean?"

"No," Gus began, but Leta broke in.

"You mean, does our house sit on pillars?"

Gus nodded.

"Yep, it does."

The basket was halfway down when the man touched his throat and yelled, "Faster, Dave, this house is about to go."

Hollis's eyes grew wide. "Go? W-what do you mean?"

Gus put his arm up, although the basket still swung far above them. "The water level is dropping. Houses knocked crooked on their pilings are breaking up." His fingers touched the basket, and he grabbed it.

With another shudder and one long, deafening *crack,* a fissure began at the front eave of the house and ran in several directions up the roof. Gus was on one side, and the children were on the other. Before anyone could move, the fissures widened and jagged sections of the house fell away. Then, the entire structure collapsed, dumping the kids into the deep, dark, water. Gus, dangling above them on his wire, managed to stay in the air. He made a swirling motion with his hand, grabbed the basket again, and dropped near the kids with a splash.

"C'mon!" he yelled, sinking the carrier into the water.

Hollis pulled Algie, who had slipped into the water next to him, into the basket first. He then waved for Leta. She paddled up and climbed in with Algie. Hollis squeezed into the basket last. He knew that the ride up would be a tight one. With a smooth jerk, the basket rose, twisting back and forth in the air. Remaining in the water, Gus watched them ascend.

Hollis laced his fingers through the wires of the transport and settled himself on the bottom of the basket as well as possible. After pushing Algie into Hollis's lap, Leta squatted in the tiny space that was left. Hollis kept his eyes fixed overhead, urging the men to pull faster. The basket seemed too light and fragile to hold them all, and the twisting that had begun when they left the water only increased as they ascended.

Algie squirmed in Hollis's lap. "I don't like this ride, Hollis. It's makin' me d-dizzy."

"Algie, sit still," Hollis exclaimed, letting go of the basket's sides and grabbing the little boy. Algie sat still for a moment and then lunged forward, trying to scramble to his feet.

"Algie!" Leta and Hollis both cried in terror.

Algie managed to get to his knees before Hollis hauled him back into his lap. The already twisting basket now swung like a pendulum.

"I wanna get down!" Algie screamed. "I don't like it!"

"Algie, stop!" Leta yelled. "You're making it worse. Sit still!"

A large hand grabbed the side of the basket, bringing it to a jolting halt. They had reached the helicopter at last. Hollis stared into the body of the chopper, but he couldn't see much.

The coast guardsman hauled the basket against the machine, attached it to a hook, and then reached in to pick up Algie. Algie twisted in the basket and threw his arms around Hollis's neck. It took Leta, Hollis, and the guardsman to pry him off. Finally, Algie let go and clapped his hands over his ears to block out the noise of the whirling blades overhead. The guardsman swung the boy under his arm like a big sack of rice. To Hollis's surprise, Algie squeezed his eyes shut and clung to the man's gray jumpsuit instead of fighting. Hollis scrambled out of the basket and put his arms out to take Algie, but the guardsman gestured for him to sit on the floor against the opposite wall.

Hollis could see much more now that he was inside the chopper. Several people were already there, sitting on the floor. One man gave him a tired smile as Hollis crawled past. Leta scooted over to join him, and the coast guardsman handed Algie back to them.

"Can you keep him still?" the man said, yelling over the noise.

Hollis shrugged. *How can I know what Algie will do in a helicopter?* The man hesitated and then nodded. To Hollis's relief, Algie stayed still and stared around with big eyes.

Gus appeared at the door and swung inside. After the other guardsman slid the door closed, the big machine moved forward with a smooth jerk. While the guardsman took the seat up front next to the pilot, Gus crawled over to sit with the three children.

Making sure we don't cause any trouble. Hollis looked at Algie, who was sneaking sideways glances at Gus. *Probably a good idea.*

"Took a swim, eh Gus?" the pilot said with a laugh.

Gus nodded but didn't speak. As Hollis watched, an intent expression crossed Gus's face, and one of his eyebrows flew up. "What?" he said, touching his earpiece. "Yeah, I know we're shut down. For the night, right?"

He listened as the person on the other end replied.

"Why completely?" Gus's voice grew sharp. "Who *cares* about looting? We're here to save people, not to stop looters." He listened for a while, and when he spoke again, he sounded subdued. "Yeah, we've heard the shooting. I don't think it was at us, but still—" He listened for a long time and then said "Out" and knocked on the back of the pilot's chair.

"What was that about?" yelled the pilot over his shoulder.

"We're shut down," Gus shouted. "Too dangerous. People on roofs are shooting at the choppers."

"You're kidding! Why?"

Gus shook his head. "Don't know. They think it might be looters trying to get us to go away or people on the roofs trying to get our attention. I can't imagine that people who want help would shoot at the people trying to help them. But who knows?"

"Nothing about this operation has gone as expected," the pilot said. "We're rewriting the book on this one."

"They're calling us in until the National Guard says the shooting is under control."

Leta and Hollis glanced at each other. "Guess we got picked up just in time," Leta whispered. "Wonder if anyone found Jonas yet."

The helicopter landed with a soft bump. With Hollis and Leta close behind, Algie followed Gus out of the chopper into a roped-off landing area. Gus ducked his head to avoid the helicopter blades. Hollis grinned as Algie copied Gus, even though the blades were far above the little boy's head.

Looking around, Hollis wondered where they were. It seemed to be a parking lot of some kind. He could just make out yellow lines on the hard black ground. Huge generator trucks with floodlights, like the ones Hollis had seen at City Park during the Christmas light show, sat here and there, providing some pools of illumination in a few patches. Everything else was dark, but Hollis could see lots of people hurrying all over the place just outside the roped-off area.

Taking Algie by the hand, Gus left the roped area and entered the crowd. Hollis grabbed Leta and, pulling her along, ran to keep up. They passed police, National Guard, and lines and lines of buses. The noise and fumes from all of the machinery battered Hollis.

"This way," Gus yelled.

The three children scurried after him. He halted outside a tent, where a large group of coast guardsmen were gathered, and crouched in front of them.

Jostled this way and that by the mass of people, Hollis made out the buildings of Lakeside Mall through the shadows. Usually bright and beckoning, the structures were dark and silent hulks squatting in the center of the lot. Gee had brought them to Lakeside Mall every Christmas to see Santa. It was crowded then, but nothing like this. Even the crowds at Mardi Gras were nothing like this.

"Where do you three have family?" Gus asked.

Hollis rubbed his head. Grammy Williams lived in Baton Rouge, but Hollis didn't know where. He'd talked to her a few times on the phone, but they hadn't been to her house since their father had left them.

"Mr. Marvin said he'd try to get Miz Jackson and Gee to Baton Rouge," Leta said.

Hollis nodded. "Baton Rouge." They could go there to find both Gee and Grammy Williams. Maybe she would even know where his father was.

"That's fine," Gus said. "You'll go to the Red Cross shelter in Baton Rouge. Your people can pick you up there." He glanced at Hollis. "You're in charge, kid. I'll go find out where the Baton Rouge bus is. Wait right here."

Hollis nodded. Gus vanished into the tent. Hollis turned back to Leta and Algie.

"Food *and* getting off the roof." He grinned. "Best birthday *ever!*"

Leta laughed and then grunted as a dark shape pushed past her, followed by two more.

"Ouch!" Algie yelped. "He stepped on my foot! Hollis!"

"Come closer to me," Hollis said. "It's so dark, no one can see us, I guess. There's a light over there. Let's go stand by it so people won't trample us to death."

"But Gus said—" Leta began.

"He'll see us. In fact, he'll see us better. It's just right over there. We can watch the front of the tent."

Hollis moved toward the light and fell over a short shape that squawked at him. Apologizing to the child and the tall shape next to it, he hustled his brother and sister to the pool of light provided by the lamp. He relaxed as people in the brightly lit area passed without running into them.

"See? This is better. Now, as soon as I see *anyone* coming out of the tent, I'll—" He was interrupted by a man in a muddy track suit running past, almost knocking him over. Before Hollis could react, the man grabbed Algie and disappeared into the crowd.

Chapter 14

Shelter-Jacked

"What the—?" Hollis sputtered. He stared at the space where his brother had been only a moment before and then glanced at Leta. "Run!" he screamed, sprinting after the man who'd vanished into the darkness.

Hollis could tell which way the man had gone because of the angry noises people made as he shoved past. Darting in the man's wake, he yelled, "Stop that man! He's got my little brother! Stop that guy!"

Suddenly, something barreled into Hollis, plowing him backward into a dimly lit clearing next to a generator truck. He was knocked back against the side of the truck with a ringing clang. It was the man, still clutching Algie under his arm. Hollis and the man stood glaring at each other, their chests heaving. With his heart battering against his ribcage, Hollis leaned against the truck for support. He wondered if the man would kill them. Algie hung like a rag doll in the man's arms, his Spongebob pajama top ripped open in the front. As Hollis watched, the little boy held an arm out toward him.

Rage flooding him, Hollis stepped away from the truck. "Give me my brother."

Her footsteps slapping the pavement, Leta appeared behind the man, who leaped to the side and held Algie like a shield. Leta halted, gasping for air.

"Go for help, Leta!" Hollis yelled.

"You don't go nowhere, Leta!" the man said. "'Less you want this little man here to get hurt."

Leta had started to turn, but she stopped at the sound of her name. Hollis beckoned her over. She scuttled across the clearing to him, tears on her cheeks.

Hollis's eyes never left the man. "What do you want with our brother?"

The man laughed. "Don' want him. *Need* him. Them rescue people? They want families on they buses. People with kids. Got no kids. Saw you in the light. Now dis kid? He my kid."

Hollis saw Leta glance his way. *My fault he got us. Leta was right. Shoulda just stayed where we were.* He studied the man so that he could describe him to the police. He was black, thin, and short. Since most of the people being rescued looked rough, Hollis didn't fault him for the patchy chin hair or the filthy track suit. The man's teeth were another story: cracked, broken, and missing. Hollis knew a drug addict when he saw one, and he knew he couldn't trust one with anything, let alone his little brother.

"You help me," the man went on, his lips twitching, "you get little man back."

Hollis considered the offer. He didn't see any alternatives. No one appeared to be coming to help them. All Hollis wanted was to get Algie and return to Gus. *We can go with him, tell the bus driver the truth, and go back to where we're s'posed to wait. Everything'll be fine.*

He nodded.

The man closed one eye and peered at Hollis. He began squeezing Algie's sides. Algie started to cry. "Seem like he bruise easy."

Leta squeaked.

"You rat, *either* of you, and he gets more than bruised. You get me in trouble, he pays."

Hollis lowered his head and nodded again. He saw the man's eyes narrow and then watched him grin.

"I'm Oscar, jus' in case they ax. Don' forget."

Hollis nodded. He had stopped fighting, but he hadn't stopped thinking. "Plan B" presented itself as the man turned away. *Get on the bus. Wait 'til he lets Algie go. Tell the bus driver to let us off.*

"Come on," he said to Leta. "We better go."

Leta wiped her nose with the top of her shirt and fell in step with Hollis behind Oscar, who led them toward one of the buses. Hollis sensed Leta looking at him, but he avoided her eye. He kept his attention on Oscar.

In charge. What a joke. "This would never, ever have happened to Jonas," he whispered to Leta.

She sniffled and patted him on the back. It made Hollis feel better. "Maybe he's getting on the Baton Rouge bus," she said.

A wild hope streaked through Hollis. "That would be perfect!"

Leta showed him her crossed fingers.

Oscar and Algie stopped in front of a middle-aged woman next to a bus loaded with people.

"These my kids," Oscar told her. "I got three, see?"

The woman frowned. "Why are they crying?"

The man shoved his face forward until he was inches from her eyes. "Look around, lady. Wouldn't you?"

After a slight hesitation, the woman stepped aside. As Oscar grinned, Hollis saw the woman grimace.

Great! Now they think this crackhead is my old man. Tears stung his eyes. *Being in charge sucks. Please, please, let this be the Baton Rouge bus.*

Air conditioning wafted over Hollis for the first time in days, causing him to shiver in his sweaty clothes. Ignoring the empty seat at the front of the bus, Oscar tromped to the only other open one, which was in the very back. Algie marched ahead of him, and when they reached the end, Oscar pushed Algie into the seat and squeezed in beside him.

Hollis and Leta waited by the front row. When Oscar gestured for them to sit down, Hollis and Leta slid into the seat behind the driver. The woman guarding the door got on the bus and sat across the aisle from Hollis and Leta.

"Thank God we're finally full," she said, her hands shaking. "Too many angry, upset people out there, and it's getting worse. Let's get out of here!"

"Don't have to tell me twice," the bus driver said.

He turned and floored the accelerator. Hollis and Leta fell backwards in the seat, while the rest of the people on the bus howled and cheered. The bus driver raised a fist like he was a champion. Hollis and Leta stared at each other in dismay.

A moment later, a tearful Algie appeared at Hollis's elbow.

"You can't run around on the bus, little boy," the woman told Algie, who was in the process of climbing over Hollis to get to a relieved Leta. He turned and stuck his tongue out at the woman.

"He won't," Hollis said, sending the woman a wobbly smile. He and Leta hugged Algie, who said he wasn't hurt.

"Aren't you going to tell them what Oscar did?" Leta whispered.

"Do you think we should? He's still here."

"There's a lot of other people here, too. They'll stop him from hurting us. They'll probably put him off the bus. That would be great!"

Hollis still hesitated. "What if they don't?"

Leta bit her lip. "At least find out where we're going."

Turning to the woman, Hollis leaned across the aisle. "Excuse me."

The woman shook her head. "Not now, little boy. This has all been terribly . . . upsetting."

"But—"

"I said, not now! I know you've been through a lot, but we've been here all day and I'm exhausted. I just can't talk right now." She turned her head away.

Undaunted, Hollis leaned forward and touched the driver on the back. "Excuse me."

"Driving!" the man said in a loud, angry voice. "Can't talk and drive! And don't touch me!"

Hollis sat back and caught Leta's expectant eye. "*You* ask them."

Leta's chin dropped and she said nothing.

"Great time for you to get shy. We'll just ride to wherever they're going, and if it ain't Baton Rouge, we'll take the bus back again. Or catch one that's going to Baton Rouge. I don't know what else to do."

Leta sighed. Leaning back in his seat, Hollis let Algie stretch across his lap to go to sleep. Leta nodded off soon after. Lulled by the comfort of the plush bus seats, Hollis soon joined them. He slept a long time— through six states.

Chapter 15

Stuck

"Little boy? Little boy?" A soft voice broke into Hollis's awareness. "Wake up. You're here."

"Here?" Hollis mumbled, stirring. A scent drifted into his nostrils. Gardenia. "Gee?" he grunted.

The voice didn't sound like Gee, but he was too excited to notice that. His eyes flew open, but Gee was not there. Yelping in surprise, he scrambled sideways and slammed into the sleeping Algie and Leta.

"Oh, honey." The wrinkled witch, who had loomed inches from his face, became an ordinary elderly lady with faded gray eyes and curls as white and shiny as his mother's good plates. She straightened up and smiled. "I didn't mean to scare you."

Hollis nodded, his hope crushed. "You smell like my grandmother," he said without enthusiasm.

"Well, that's very nice," she said. "It must be the perfume my grandchildren bought for my birthday."

Leta and Algie sat up rubbing their faces. Hollis moved over to give them room. "Where are we?"

"You're at First Methodist Church in Charleston," she said.

Hollis frowned. That didn't sound like Baton Rouge.

"*South Carolina?*" Leta squeaked.

"No, dear," the lady said. "West Virginia."

Hollis tried to remember where West Virginia was.

"I gotta pee," Algie said. "Is West Virginia in B-Baton Rouge?"

"No, dear," the lady said.

"It's by Ohio, Algie," Leta said.

Hollis tried to think of where Ohio was.

"You know your geography, don't you, dear?" the lady said to Leta, who looked smug and nodded.

Of course she does. Hollis gave up trying to figure out where they were. He'd ask Leta later.

"There's a bathroom on the bus," the lady told Algie. "But if you can wait just a moment, I'll take you to a nicer one inside."

Algie nodded, and they got up. Hollis noticed that the bus was empty. Everyone else must have gotten off while they slept. Shading his eyes from the overhead sun, he estimated it to be about lunch time. Following the others off the bus, he hurried to catch up to the lady before they entered the shelter.

"What time is it?" he asked.

"About noon," she said.

"Lunch time! Good! I'm starving," Leta said.

"What time does the bus go back?" Hollis asked.

The woman appeared confused. "Back where?"

"Back to New Orleans. We have to go back."

"Well, it's dangerous there. The bus isn't going back. This was our last run. The shelter is full."

Hollis stared. "No," he said. "We have to go back! A man kidnapped Algie and made us get on the bus with him. That was the only way they'd let him on. We have to go to Baton Rouge. Our grandmother is there."

"My goodness! Do you know where this man is now?"

"I guess he's in there." Hollis pointed at the shelter. "Once the bus left New Orleans, he let us go."

"Well, don't worry about him anymore. We all knew you had to be here without a parent when everyone else got off the bus and no one woke you up. But we can't send you back to New Orleans. How about we get in touch with your grandmother and send you to where she is. Would that be okay?"

Hollis hesitated before nodding. *Maybe I haven't screwed up as bad as I thought.*

They entered a long white hallway with fluorescent lighting. A few steps brought them to a pair of gray doors, one marked "Men" and the other "Women."

"There you go," she said. "I'm Miss Violet. What are your names?"

Unexpected tears gathered in the corners of Hollis's eyes. "Your name is pretty," he said. "It was our mama's name. She died of cancer four years ago."

Miss Violet patted his shoulder. "I'm so sorry, dear. We'll try to get you back to your grandmother as quickly as we can."

Leta held out her hand. "I'm Leta," she said. "That's Hollis and Algie."

"Well, Leta, I'll go in this one with you, and Hollis, you and Algie go in the other."

The bathroom was huge, and both boys hurried to make use of the facilities. Some men stood at the sinks, washing themselves and shaving, but there were fewer than Hollis had expected. He scanned the room for Oscar, but he wasn't there. Once Hollis was finished, he made Algie wash his hands in the same sink he had used. They rejoined Miss Violet and Leta in the hallway.

"Now," said Miss Violet, "let's get some lunch."

Algie glared. "You got any red beans? Or cabbage?"

Miss Violet smiled. "No, but I'm sure we can do better for you than beans and cabbage."

"No, you can't, 'cause—'cause—I'm n-not hungry." Scowling, Algie folded his arms and tucked his chin to his chest.

"You *must* be after that long ride. We're having Margie's tuna noodle casserole. You'll love it."

Algie's mouth dropped open. "I d-don't like tuna noodle . . . a-anythin'. I'm not eatin' unless Gee cooks."

Leta frowned. "You've never had tuna noodle casserole, Algie. None of us has."

"Yeah, well, I d-don't want to," he said, his brows drawn together and his mouth set.

"You ate an MRE," Hollis reminded him. "Gee didn't cook that."

"That was soldier food. I wish I was b-back on the roof. I n-never got to eat my soldier candy!"

"Hush, Algie. You're being rude," Leta said. "He's sorry, Miss Violet."

"No, I'm not."

Miss Violet laughed. "I'm sure we'll find something he'll want to eat."

Hollis lifted his fork to the level of his nose and gave it a sniff. Secretly, he felt the same way as Algie about trying Margie's tuna noodle casserole. Taking a tiny bit onto the end of his tongue, he rolled it around in his mouth. Across the table, Algie watched, his forehead and nose wrinkled and his mouth turned down.

"Something wrong with your peanut butter?" Hollis asked.

Algie threw down his untasted sandwich. "I'm not gonna eat it."

Hollis shrugged and took another tentative bite.

"So what d-does it taste like?" Algie asked, his expression suggesting that Hollis was eating roaches.

"It's good," Hollis said. Setting his shoulders, he put the entire fork-full into his mouth and swallowed right away. *It really ain't bad.* He dug his fork in again. "It's very creamy and only a little fishy. I like fish anyway."

"Well I don't," Algie stated. "And I don't like peanut butter either."

Miss Violet's forehead wrinkled. "I think we have some SPAM someone donated." Her chair scraped the floor as she rose to find out.

"No!" Algie screamed.

"No, thank you," Hollis told her. "That's okay."

Miss Violet sat down again.

"Oh, Algie," Leta whispered to him. "You like peanut butter. *And* fish. And SPAM, too. You're just being stubborn."

"Leave him alone," Hollis whispered as well. "He'll get hungry at some point and eat."

Algie shook his head.

Leta looked doubtful, but she dropped the subject.

Hollis took a sip from his chocolate milk carton and eyed the other people in the room. Spotting Oscar, he leaned over to Miss Violet.

"That's Oscar. He's the man who stole Algie," he said, pointing with his fork.

Miss Violet glanced over at the man. "I hate to turn anyone away. You've all been through so much—him included. He didn't actually *hurt* Algie, did he?"

Hollis glared at Oscar, who was shoveling Margie's tuna noodle casserole into his face like it was trying to swim away. "He scared him and he tore his pajamas. He scared all of us."

Leta, who had been listening, leaned forward. "He also *took* Algie from us. If we hadn't followed, who knows what would have happened?"

Miss Violet looked over at Algie, who was shredding his smashed sandwich. "Okay. Wait right here." She got up and walked across the room to where Oscar was sitting.

"What's she doing?" Leta gasped.

"I don't know." Hollis said.

"She's talkin' to him," Leta said, her voice squeaking. She clutched Hollis's arm. "She's bringin' him over." Miss Violet had moved to return to their table, and Oscar rose to join her.

"No she's not. She's not *that* stupid." Miss Violet escorted Oscar back to his seat. He looked over at Leta and Hollis and grinned. Then he mouthed, "Sorry."

"He's *sorry*?" Leta said. "Does he think that's gonna change anything?"

"When she gets back, we need to tell her to call the police," Hollis said.

Leta nodded.

Miss Violet slid back into her seat across from the children. "He says he's very sorry for frightening you. He says that none of the buses would let him on and he was desperate. He says that he knew you would follow and that he wanted you to follow."

"He's lyin'! He ran into the crowd to lose us. Then when we caught him, he threatened us! Can't you call the police or *something*?"

Miss Violet bit her lip. "But he didn't keep Algie. And, he got you here, where we can help you. I could call the police, but I just think he's been through a terrible time too. He certainly looks like he has."

Miss Violet turned to Algie. "What do you think, Algie?"

"'Bout what?"

"About calling the police about the man who grabbed you." She took the pieces of sandwich out of his hand and removed the plate, then wiped his fingers with her napkin.

Algie watched her cleaning his hands, and a tear started down his cheek. "I-I just wanna g-go home."

Miss Violet wiped the tear away, too. "How about this. We'll keep an eye on him," she said, "I've told him to stay away from you and not to even speak to you again. If he does, then come straight to me and let me know. *Then* we'll call the police, I promise. Meanwhile, I'll try to find your family, Hollis, and another place for Oscar to go."

Hollis and Leta brightened a bit at the last part of what she said.

"I guess so," Leta said, looking at Hollis.

"Can you find him something quick?" Hollis asked.

"I'll try," said Miss Violet. "Now, how did you three get separated from your grandmother?"

"The Coast Guard man said we couldn't fit in the boat, but they took Gee because of her diabetes," Leta said. "Mr. Marvin said he was gonna get his wife, Miz Jackson, and Gee to a hospital in Baton Rouge, and the Coast Guard man, Gus, said he'd put us on a Baton Rouge bus. If Oscar hadn't grabbed Algie, we'd be there like we're supposed to be. And Gee was unconscious when they took her. I—I hope she's woken up by now."

"Well, I'm going to take care of Oscar," Miss Violet said. "So let's focus on how we can get you to your grandmother. I'm going to call every hospital in Baton Rouge. Unless you know one that they'd go to?"

Leta shook her head.

"Oh, well. There can't be that many. We'll have you there in no time."

"Thanks, Miss Violet." Hollis said, smiling at her.

Chapter 16

The Others

After lunch, Miss Violet brought them into a huge meeting room filled with cots and people. She told them that about a hundred people were being housed there. Overwhelmed, Hollis trailed after her and stared around at the crowd in the room. *This must be a really big church.*

They came to an area separated from the main section. Several children sat playing with toys by a small knot of cots, which were clustered together by a table, a couch, and a TV with a Nintendo and a DVD player.

"These children are here without their parents, too," Miss Violet said. "We ask that the children without parents stay separate from the other people and families in the shelter, so this area is all yours." She turned and called, "Eden! We've got some new kids for you."

A tall girl rose and eyed the three of them. She was very pretty, with cinnamon-colored skin, light green eyes, and hair piled up in a curly mass on top of her head. *Jonas will be sorry he missed meeting this girl.* One by one, the rest of the kids stopped playing and straggled over to see the latest additions.

"This is Algie, Leta, and Hollis. They came in this morning," said Miss Violet. She turned to them. "Okay, I'm going to leave you here now to get to know each other while I go call some hospitals, right Hollis? What's your grandmother's name?"

"Gee Gaudet," Hollis said. "G-a-u-d-e-t."

"Thank you. As soon as I hear something, I'll let you know." She strolled away, nodding to some women waving at her.

Hollis turned and viewed the other kids.

"Y'all got funny names," the tallest boy said, curling his lip. "Algie—ha, ha! Where'd they get you? Outta a fish bowl?"

The other children laughed or hid smiles. Eden rolled her eyes.

"Our names ain't funny," Hollis said, bristling. "What's yours, anyway?"

The boy's chest swelled. "Maleeki."

Hollis flopped forward at the waist, shaking with exaggerated laughter. "You leaky? That's where all that water came from?" he howled.

The others burst out laughing, even Eden. Maleeki balled up his hands and took a step forward. Hollis stopped laughing and brought up his own fists. Algie ran between the two boys toward the strangers. He had spotted a tiny girl hiding behind an older girl's leg. The would-be combatants glared at each other but dropped their fists.

"W-who are you?" Algie, entranced, asked the little girl.

The child edged away, pressing against the older girl, who leaned over and said, "Go on. Tell him."

The little girl buried her face against the older girl's leg.

"All right," the older girl said. "This is Loquisha and I'm her sister, Tameka. But you can call us Lolo and Kiki like everyone else. I'm fourteen and Lolo is four. Maleeki is our cousin. He's eleven."

Hollis smiled. *Good. I'm older than Maleeki.*

"This," Kiki went on, "is Eden. She's sixteen and the oldest—"

Eden interrupted her. "I may be the oldest, but Kiki is the bossiest."

Kiki glared at her but went on. "The two over there are Drayden and Calaya. They're both ten. They aren't related to anybody."

"You can call me Dray," Drayden piped up.

"Well," Leta said, "I'm nine and Hollis is twelve and Algie is five. I think he likes you, Lolo."

Lolo hid her face again.

Hollis realized he was the oldest boy. *Good. No Jonas to get in the way.* He immediately felt guilty for thinking that when he didn't know what had happened to his brother. Smiling at the others, he asked, "Where do y'all live?"

"You mean where *did* we live, don't you?" Eden asked, staring down her nose at Hollis. "It's underwater now. We lived in the East. On Stillwater."

Calaya spoke up. "I lived out there, too. On Cerise." She sat down on the floor, and the other children followed, forming a loose circle.

All of the others were from the New Orleans East area, as Hollis had suspected. He knew a lot of kids in the Ninth Ward, but he'd never seen any of these children before.

"So where you go to school?" Dray asked.

"Martin Luther," Hollis said. Leta nodded.

"You play football?"

"Yeah," Hollis said, looking him over.

"Calaya, Maleeki, and I go to Williams Middle. Eden and Kiki go to Abramson High."

The other children chimed in, comparing favorite restaurants, movie theaters, and shopping centers.

After a pause, Dray said, "I can't believe it's all gone."

Everyone got quiet and sad until Leta spoke up again. "We don't know where our family is. Our big brother Jonas swam off to save people, and we never saw him again."

"Think he's dead?" Maleeki asked, his eyes wide.

Hollis shook his head, even though he'd wondered the same thing. "He's a good swimmer."

"Don't matter, though," Dray said. "Might get bit by a snake or a gator in that water."

"You saw gators?" Maleeki asked Dray, his eyes growing wider.

Dray shook his head. "I'm just sayin'. There *might* be some."

"He had an axe," Hollis said. "He wouldn't be worried about no gator."

"What's he doin' with an axe?" Kiki asked.

"Getting people out of their houses," Hollis told her. "Chopping through the roof. It's what he did to ours."

Maleeki snorted. "Yeah, right. Lootin's more like it. Breakin' *into* people's houses."

Hollis rose to his knees. "Take that back. Jonas wouldn't steal. Take it back, or I'll pound you."

Maleeki laughed and rolled backwards onto the floor. "I'm just jokin' with you."

"Besides," Kiki said. "Maleeki can't talk. He steals."

"I do not!" Maleeki yelled, sitting up.

"He does," she insisted. "He sure does. You watch your things around him."

"What things?" Algie asked.

Everyone laughed at first, because of how true it was, but Eden quickly sobered.

"It's really not funny," she said. "Losin' everything."

The rest of the group lost their smiles as well, and Hollis thought about his Game Boy. It had taken all of his Christmas money and most of what he'd made that summer mowing lawns to buy it. Now it was gone. He could tell that the rest of the group was thinking of things they'd lost. Everyone but Maleeki. He still sat with his arms folded and an angry expression on his face.

"They took our grandmother away in a boat because of her diabetes," Leta said. "I hope she's all right."

"My momma has sugar, too," Dray said. "I hope they helped her at that parking lot we was in."

Eden glanced at Calaya, who appeared to be about to cry. "Calaya lives with her grandmama, but she spent the night with her auntie. Now she doesn't know what happened to her grandmama, do you, Calaya?"

Calaya shook her head and began to sob with loud snorts and gasps. Leta hopped up and started across the room toward the shelter office. She got about three steps away before Kiki caught up to her.

"Don't go anywhere by yourself, Leta," Hollis heard Kiki say. "We all go around in twos and threes. There might be bad people here. Don't even go to the bathroom alone at night. Wake up one of us. We'll go with you."

Leta's eyes grew wide and she nodded. "I didn't think about that," she said. "I wanted to get some tissue for Calaya."

"Dray's got it."

Leta watched as Dray handed a roll of toilet paper to Calaya.

"All them people are strangers," Kiki said, glaring at the other part of the shelter. "One thing bad people do is try to get you to trust them. Then they hurt you."

Leta nodded. "We already know one bad man."

"Really?" Kiki asked, eyes wide. "You have to tell us about him. But first we need to go see Miss Violet to get y'all some cots put over here."

Some men with T-shirts that read "First Methodist Church, We Care!" set up cots for Hollis, Leta, and Algie. Miss Violet gave them each a towel, a washcloth, a roll of toilet paper, and something she called a "goody box." Hollis opened his small cardboard box and found candy, cards, a pencil, a pen, a puzzle book, and an apple.

While the men finished setting up the cots, Miss Violet took the three kids to a sheet-covered table along the back wall that held all kinds of clothing, sorted by sizes. Other tables, piled high with items donated for the evacuees, lay along the walls around the rest of the room.

"We have to get you out of those pajamas," Miss Violet said to Algie, who surveyed his torn top. "Aren't you sick of them?"

Algie shook his head. "C-can't we w-wash them?"

Miss Violet laughed, and Leta shook her head. "If we wash them, Algie, they'll fall apart."

Algie frowned.

"Maybe we can get you some new ones," Miss Violet said. "I'll keep an eye out for a set. Now, find yourselves some things to wear." She disappeared into another room.

Hollis and Leta checked the sizes on the table in front of them, pulling out items they thought would fit each of them. Soon, they each had a small stack of clothing.

When Miss Violet returned, her arms were filled with packs of socks and underwear. They thanked her and, loaded down with their new possessions, headed back to their cots. Along the way, Algie gave a sudden crow, dropped everything he'd been given, and ran over to another donation table.

"Algie! Come back!" Leta cried.

She and Hollis struggled to pick up his things. Algie returned, his chest puffed with pride. In his arms nestled a two-foot polyresin figure, adorned with a fluffy white beard and dressed in a yellow shirt and a pointed red hat.

Hollis eyed the garden gnome, appalled. "Put that back."

Algie shook his head. "I like him."

Leta laughed. "He's just like the ones at Mr. Joseph's house."

Algie glared at Hollis from behind the red hat. "I'm bringing him to Gee for the yard. His name is Gnomie."

Miss Violet smiled. "You never know what you'll find in donations."

Algie snuggled his cheek against the gnome's hat.

Leta whispered, "Maybe he'll make Algie easier to handle."

"You think one of us ought to remind him there's no yard anymore?" Hollis waved his hand. "Whatever. If it makes him happy."

The three thanked Miss Violet and wobbled back to their cots. When they had almost reached their area, a huge man, tall and dark, appeared and squatted in front of them, blocking their way.

"Hi," he rumbled in a deep, rich voice. "Nice gnome." He patted Gnomie's hat.

Algie grinned.

"My name's Red. You can call me Red Beans. I'm not gonna bother you three for long. I'm just gonna tell you what I've told the other kids. If you have any trouble from any of these people, you come let me know. I'll take care of it. Okay?"

Hollis nodded, his chin disappearing into the clothing he held. The man got up and ambled away.

"Who's th-that?" Algie asked, wide-eyed.

"He's really big," Leta said. "Do we trust him?"

Hollis stared after Red Beans. "We'll ask Eden."

"Maybe he's trying to get us to trust him so he can do something to us, like Kiki was saying," Leta said.

Hollis nodded. "I say we stay away."

"Do we tell Miss Violet?"

Hollis shook his head. The man hadn't done anything yet, and he knew what Miss Violet would say about that. He'd tell if something happened. "Stay away from him, Algie, okay?"

Algie frowned. "I l-like him. He l-looks like F-fat Albert and, anyway, I l-like red beans."

Hollis considered that. "He *does* look like Fat Albert, but he ain't Fat Albert. Stay away."

Algie scowled but nodded. Hollis sighed. He hoped that Miss Violet would find Gee soon, before anything—or anyone—got in their way. Being an adult was much more complicated than he'd thought.

Chapter 17

Dead Ends

Two days passed with no word from Miss Violet about Gee's location. Oscar hadn't left yet, either. Hollis set aside his thoughts on Oscar and concentrated on Gee. He felt both bored and scared. There was no way that Jonas or Gee could find them way out in West Virginia. Leta had drawn a rough map of the country, and so Hollis now had a good idea how far away they'd driven from New Orleans. Right now, Miss Violet was their only hope. He wanted to find some way he could help her.

The families in the shelter gathered at the door to the dining area in anticipation of lunch. Before leaving the kids area, Hollis glanced at the TV, which showed the mayhem still going on in New Orleans. Lines of people had just been discovered at the convention center. They were screaming, begging for someone to come get them. Hollis was glad that he wasn't still there but wondered if Jonas was among those remaining.

"I don't see Jonas," Leta said from her cot. "I've been watching and watching. So many people are still stuck there."

"Yeah," Hollis said. "And we're still stuck here. Lunch, Leta. Algie?"

"No!" Algie said.

Hollis started toward him, but Algie jumped up and ran past him to join the line now filing out to eat. Smiling, Hollis was about to follow when he spotted the toe of a Nike sticking out from underneath Maleeki's bed. The toe stirred and slowly drew out of sight beneath the cot.

What's he up to?

Hollis strolled to a nearby donation table and ducked under the floor-length cloth. He lay flat on the floor, but he couldn't see Maleeki's hiding place from where he was. Just as well. If he couldn't see Maleeki, then Maleeki couldn't see him. Hollis relaxed against the floor and waited.

Not long after, he heard the sound of faint grunting and watched as Maleeki popped into view, his eyes darting around the quiet room. Once he was sure that no one remained, Maleeki crept across to the main section and slid a hand under the pillow of the nearest cot.

Hollis frowned. The low-hanging tablecloth covering the donation table was great for hiding, but not very good for spying. He sat up, trying to find a spot with a better view. A gap in the cloth at the end caught his attention. Scooting down to it, he placed his eye at the opening.

Having moved on from the first cot, Maleeki rummaged through another resident's possessions and then another. With well-practiced movements, his long fingers slipped into bags, boxes, and bedding. Arms and pockets filled at last, Maleeki hurried back to his own cot and dumped the loot into a carry-on bag Hollis had seen him get out of donations the day before. Once he had stowed away the stolen items, Maleeki shoved the bag back under his cot. With a satisfied grin and a whistled song, he sauntered off toward the dining room for lunch.

When Maleeki's whistle faded, Hollis emerged from his hiding place and scrambled over to Maleeki's cot. Yanking out the bag, he trotted with it to the family section of the shelter. After unzipping the bag, he upended it over one of the cots. Seven packs of cigarettes, three lighters, several packs of gum and candy, a pocket knife, a lady's watch, a few coins, and a ten-dollar bill fell onto the bedding.

Hands shaking, Hollis ran back to Maleeki's bed and shoved the bag underneath. He grabbed a T-shirt from the donation table and threw it over the heap of items on the other cot. He stood for a moment, his chest heaving, and surveyed the job he'd completed. Although he felt like whistling himself, he chose a quieter exit, trotting across the room and slipping into the dining area to join the others for lunch.

"Where were you?" Leta asked as Hollis slid into the seat next to her. He scanned the room and was relieved to see Maleeki sitting alone on the other side of the room with his back to their table.

"Bathroom," Hollis said and stuffed his hot dog into his mouth. He wanted to be the first one back to the resident area. French fries and a wedge of apple pie followed the hot dog. Wiping his mouth with his shirt, Hollis left Leta to finish her dessert. Algie was busy offering his hot dog to his gnome.

After jogging across the room to his bed, Hollis sat down to watch as the other residents trickled back. One man began tearing his bed apart.

"Where's my smokes?" he demanded in a loud voice.

"Mine're gone too," his wife said as she turned back her sheets and searched under her pillow. "And my lighter."

An uproar ensued as people checked their bags and discovered their losses. A man in a dirty blue shirt entered and wandered over to his bed, glancing around in curiosity at the commotion. Hollis's eyes sparkled and he sat up straighter.

When the man reached his cot, he stopped short, his face puckered in annoyance. Bending over, he yanked the shirt off the bed, revealing the small pile of treasure underneath. He froze, arm in the air, mouth open in surprise.

"That's my lighter," yelled another man. He stomped over and snatched a red lighter from the pile. "Right here. Y'all come see. Oscar's got a buncha stuff on his bed."

Oscar held up his hands and backed away from the cot. "I never took nothin'," he said. "I don't know how all that got there."

Leta strolled up, towing a scowling Algie with his gnome dragging behind him. Focused on the scene at Oscar's cot, Hollis barely acknowledged them. People came from all over the room, identified their belongings, and glared at Oscar.

"Someone's settin' me up," Oscar protested, his eyes wide and child-like. "I never took any of that stuff. And if I did," his eyes narrowed, "I'd've hidden it better. If I'd known there was stuff under there, I wouldn't have picked that shirt up, now would I?"

The man who had taken back the ten-dollar bill nodded. "I can't prove this is mine," he said, waving the bill in the air. "But Oscar never argued. He just let me have it. Maybe it was a prank."

Others nodded their agreement. Once all the items had been

returned, the people who had reclaimed their possessions drifted back to their own spaces. However, Hollis noticed that some people still threw sidelong glances at Oscar, who sat grumbling on his cot. From his cot, Hollis heard more than one person mutter, "Need to watch that guy."

"I guess he's in trouble again," Leta said.

Algie clutched Gnomie to his chest. "He's a b-bad man."

Hollis saw Maleeki scowling into his now empty bag. Maleeki lifted his head and scanned the room, raking each person with fierce, suspicious eyes. Hollis turned his head and tried to appear as innocent as possible.

Right before dinner, Miss Violet came to find Hollis, Algie, and Leta.

"Children, come with me, please," she said, her eyes unhappy as she pressed her mouth into a straight line.

Hollis glanced at Leta, who bit her lip. Algie picked up Gnomie and grabbed Leta's shirt. Looking uncertain, they all followed Miss Violet to her office. Once they had reached it, she held the door open for them.

"Algie, why don't you and Gnomie wait outside," said Miss Violet.

Algie pressed his face against Gnomie's hard, blue vest. "No."

"You might as well let him stay," Hollis said, leaning against the desk. "He'll just start screamin' if we make him leave."

Miss Violet closed the door. "Sit down, children. I have some news for you, but I'm afraid it isn't very good."

They sat on the couch. Since there was no room for Gnomie, Algie set him on the floor and clutched the peak of his red cone hat in both hands.

Miss Violet sighed and leaned back in her chair. "I've called every hospital and shelter in Baton Rouge, and then in the rest of the state of Louisiana. No one has seen your grandmother or your brother or the Jacksons. Now wait," she said, putting her hand up, her gaze directed at Algie.

Hollis noticed Algie's face clouding up to cry. He picked up Gnomie and handed him to Algie, who seized him and wildly rocked him back and forth. Leta pressed herself deeper into the couch to avoid being impaled on the tip of Gnomie's hat.

Her eyes still on Algie, Miss Violet went on, "It's good news that your brother's not in any of the hospitals, don't you think?"

Algie and Leta looked at Hollis, who sniffed and nodded. "But Gee?" Hollis asked.

"I spoke to a woman at one of the hospitals who said that the Baton Rouge hospitals filled up right away. To make sure everyone could find a doctor, they went on what they call "diversion." That means that anyone else who wanted to come to Baton Rouge had to go somewhere else instead."

"Where?" Hollis asked.

Miss Violet held up her hands. "Everywhere. The National Guard, state troopers, and police took people all over the country by helicopter, car, bus, ambulance, and sometimes airplane."

"So there's no way we can find out where Gee and Miz Jackson went?"

"I just think it's going to take a bit more time," Miss Violet said hesitantly.

Algie frowned. "W-we can't find Gee?"

"Not yet, Algie. But we're gonna keep lookin'." Leta patted Algie's arm.

A distressed expression crossed Miss Violet's face. "I know that this isn't what you were looking to hear, but I wanted to let you know where we had started to search. I know you thought we'd find her right away. We all did."

Laying his forehead on Gnomie's belly, Algie began to wail. Leta glanced at Miss Violet in embarrassment, who came around from her desk and knelt in front of Algie.

"I'll find her, Algie. Don't worry."

Algie wailed louder. "I want Gee."

Leta stroked his head and shushed him. Hollis stood up. He felt like crying too, but pride wouldn't let him do it in front of a stranger.

Leta rose, lifted Gnomie out of Algie's lap, and pulled him to his feet. After she had handed Gnomie to Hollis, she turned to Miss Violet. With her head tilted back and her nose in the air, Leta reminded Hollis of Gee when she talked to the preacher at church.

"I'm sure you'll find her, Miss Violet."

"I'm so sorry, Leta."

Leta smiled, maintaining her grown-up air, and held the still howling Algie in front of her. "I'm not worried. Come on, Algie. Stop that noise. You're upsetting Gnomie. We'll find Gee." Her voice cracked. "It's just going to take longer than we thought."

"Is there another family member somewhere that I can call?" Miss Violet asked, tapping her phone with a pencil.

Leta and Hollis glanced at one another. "There's our father's mom, Grammy Williams, in Baton Rouge, but—"

"What's her first name?"

"Mary," Hollis said. "But I don't know her number. We don't talk to her much."

"Mary Williams. I bet there are two or three of those in Baton Rouge. Do you know her address?"

Hollis shook his head. "We've never visited her. Just letting us talk to her upsets Gee. Grammy Williams says bad things about Mama. Gee doesn't like her."

"We don't like her either," said Algie, his cheeks splotchy, and he started to cry again. Leta shushed him.

Hollis watched Leta march Algie out of the office. As he followed, he said over his shoulder, "Thank you for tellin' us, Miss Violet." With head down and shoulders drooping, he scuffed his way out, Gnomie tucked under his arm.

Since Algie was still wailing when they entered the residence area, everyone knew they'd gotten bad news. Eden and Kiki met them in the children's section. Calaya and Drayden quit watching TV with Lolo and hurried over to hear the latest.

"They can't find my mom and dad either," Eden told Algie. "Or Dray's grandma or any of our parents. We don't know where our families are, just like you. And we're not crying."

"Even though we might want to," Dray added. When Eden glared at him, he stuck his tongue out at her.

"Come on, Algie." Kiki pulled on his hand. "Come watch TV with Lolo. Spongebob is on. Gnomie told me you love Spongebob."

Hiccups replaced Algie's wailing, but tears still streamed down his cheeks. Spongebob could fix a lot, but not everything.

Chapter 18

Families

The day after Miss Violet told them about not finding Gee, Hollis stood next to Eden's cot and watched her fold some of her latest finds from the donation pile. Donations arrived several times a day, and Eden was always the first person to sort through the newest items.

"Do you trust Miss Violet?" Hollis asked.

Eden looked at him in surprise. "Don't you?"

Hollis shrugged. "Just some things she does sometimes make me not."

"Like what?" Eden asked, as she quit her folding.

"Well, how we got here, a man, Oscar, that guy over there—"

"The thief?"

Hollis smiled to himself and nodded. "He stole Algie and scared him and threatened us, but she let him stay."

Eden nodded. "That doesn't surprise me."

Hollis stared at her.

"Y'see, Miss Violet? She's churchy. You know what I mean by that?"

Hollis shook his head.

"She's not a disaster-relief worker, so she really doesn't know what she's doin'. She's just a member of this church. A volunteer. One of the other volunteers told me that Katrina was so bad and happened so fast, no one was ready. The people here just want to help. Anyway, Miss Violet? She wants to help everybody. The good thing about that is she'll work really hard to find our families. The bad part is that she'll work just as hard to help people who don't care about anyone but themselves. But I think she'll do a good job for us, Hollis, I really do."

"Okay," Hollis said. "So, you have a mom and a dad?" he asked.

She nodded. "Doesn't everybody?"

Hollis shook his head, clearing a space on her bed and sitting down. "I don't. My dad left us." He held up a round box printed with a flowered pattern. "Hey! Where'd you find this?"

"Where do you think?" Eden laughed. "That's—"

"Dusting powder, I know. Gardenia—it's Gee's favorite. Is there any more? I'd like to take her some."

"You can have it. I've got lots of smell-good." Her expression changed. "You have a dad, Hollis. He just doesn't live with you. When's the last time you saw him?"

Hollis frowned. "I was six."

"That's a long time."

"That's when our mom died, too."

Eden reached out and touched his shoulder. "He left after your mom died?"

"He left before."

Eden blinked. "Are you *sure* you want to find him?"

Hollis nodded. "Everyone asks me that, but he's part of me. I want to know who he is."

"But you don't know where he is?"

Hollis's eyes grew sad. "He might be dead, for all I know."

Scanning the room, Eden laughed. "He might be here, for all you know! Would you recognize him if you saw him?"

Hollis's eyes widened. "I-I don't know." He rubbed his chin. "Gee got rid of his pictures after Mama died. Didn't want reminders of a 'no-good man who deserted us.'"

"I don't blame her."

Hollis glared at her, but his face grew thoughtful again. "He was tall and thin, with black eyes and a big smile underneath a bushy mustache."

"What if the mustache was gone? Would you know him then?"

Hollis thought for a moment. "I don't know. I was six."

As he watched her tuck her new things into a suitcase, he remembered something else he wanted to ask. "Eden, have you met Mr. Red Beans?"

Eden snorted. "That name! He came up to me when I first got here. He said if I needed anything to tell him."

"He told us that, too. Do you think he's . . . um . . . trustable?"

Eden laughed. "Trustworthy? I don't know. He never said anything to us again. I stay away from all them people. You never know."

Hollis left her to her work, but her suggestion that his father could be at the shelter had captured his imagination. He spent some time wandering around the room, peering at each of the men he passed. After receiving a suspicious look from one man who caught him staring, Hollis gave up and sought out Leta. When he found her, she was having her hair braided by Calaya.

"Do you remember Dad?" he asked her.

She wrinkled her forehead. "A little," she said at last.

Hollis's face brightened. "Do you think you'd know him if you saw him again?"

She shrugged. "Maybe, but I'm not sure. It's been a long time. I was only four. Why?"

Hollis waved at the room. "Dad could be here, and we wouldn't know it."

Leta tried to look around the room, but Calaya pulled her head back.

"Ow!" Leta turned and glared at her.

"Sit still!" Calaya told her. "You're gonna make me mess up."

Facing forward again, Leta said, "I don't think he's here, Hollis. Gee says Dad looks just like Jonas, and no one here looks like him." She bit her lip and shook her head, earning an exasperated grunt from Calaya. "It'd be too weird if he was."

Calaya glanced at Hollis and twisted a lock of Leta's hair into a tight roll against her scalp. "I know how y'all feel. I don't remember either of my parents. I've lived with my grandmama all my life."

"Where did your parents go?" Leta asked.

"Got me. My grandmama just says they're dead. She won't tell me what happened. She says that it was a long time ago and that I should let the dead sleep, but my cousin told me that they died doing drugs."

Hollis asked, "Do you miss them?"

"I never knew them," Calaya snapped. "My grandmama says, 'How can you miss someone you never met?'"

"But do you?" Hollis persisted.

Tears welled in Calaya's eyes and overflowed onto her cheeks. She kept working on Leta's hair.

"Yeah," she said at last. "I don't say anythin', because it makes my grandmama upset. I guess it isn't so much that I miss them as it is I wanna know what they like."

"Even if they're bad people, right?" Hollis tilted his head.

Calaya puffed up and glared at Hollis, ready to defend her family, but nodded all the same.

"Yeah," Hollis said. "Our dad is s'posed to be a bad guy, but I still want to know him. It would make Gee mad if I said that, so I don't talk about it. She doesn't understand."

"Maybe she understands more than you think," Leta said. "If Gee says we don't need to know Dad, that's good enough for me." Lowering her voice, she asked, "But Hollis? What if Gee is dead?"

Calaya met Hollis's eyes over Leta's head and raised her brows.

Hollis stared at Calaya and then at Leta. *What if? I can't even think about that.*

Leta went on. "What if Jonas *and* Gee are dead and we're all alone? What's gonna happen to us?"

Calaya snorted. "I can tell you that. Foster care. They was gonna put me in that stupid, loser system if my grandmama hadn't said she'd take me. You don't wanna be in that."

Leta frowned. "Maybe you're right, Hollis. Maybe we need to find Dad in case that's true. I don't see Grammy Williams taking us. And Algie? He's not doing so good."

Before Hollis could ask Leta what she meant about Algie, Dray and Kiki wandered over and joined them.

"What y'all talkin' about?" Dray asked, gazing at Calaya's tears with concern. He reached out and patted her arm.

"Families," Leta said.

"Oh." Dray let his hand drop. "No *wonder* everyone's cryin'. I sure miss my grandma."

Calaya sniffled and smiled. "You live with your grandmama, too?" He nodded.

"Where are your parents?"

"They around," he said. "I see them when I want."

"Why don't you live with them?" Hollis asked.

"They got divorced and married new people. I didn't like that. I wanted them to stay with each other. First I lived with Mama and Harold. He tried to be my dad, always orderin' me around. He and I argued a bunch, and he told Mama it was him or me. She picked him. So I went with Dad and Phoenicia." Dray said the name in a high, whiny voice, placing a hand on his waist and swinging his hips. Kiki covered her mouth to keep from laughing.

"All Phoenicia cared about were *her* kids. She had three. Her oldest boy was three years older than me. I used to beat him stupid."

"Why?" Hollis asked. "Was he mean?"

"No," Dray said. "He was straight. I don't know why I hit him all the time. Maybe 'cause I couldn't hit *her*. Anyway, the third time I beat him up, Dad sent me to live with Grandma. Everythin' got better. My grandma is *gangsta*!"

"How did you get here without her?" Leta asked.

Dray's face fell. "I lost her in the crowd at Lakeside Mall. Saw someone from the back that looked like her. It was that lady over there."

He pointed and the children saw an elderly black woman tottering toward the shelter bathrooms.

"That lady got on the bus, and I ran over and told the driver my grandma was on his bus, and he let me on. By the time I realized it wasn't her, the bus was leaving and the driver told me to sit down and be quiet. He wouldn't let me off."

Calaya nodded. "I was on that bus, Dray. I saw you get upset. My grandmama went to the hospital the week before the storm, so I was stayin' with my auntie. I lost her in the crowd too, and I was so scared to be alone that I got on the first bus I saw."

"Kiki, Lolo, and Maleeki were there," said Dray. "A National Guard guy put their parents on one bus and put them on the bus to come here. He said the busses were goin' to the same place. They weren't."

"That's so stupid. Why would he do that?" Leta asked.

"'Cause he didn't give a care," Maleeki said, sauntering up. "None of them did."

"There was a lot of stuff goin' on," Dray said. "He mighta got confused. He was mean, though. Yellin' and wavin' at everyone, like he was all mad at us."

"He scared Lolo," Kiki said. "He grabbed her and set her on the stairs to the bus and yelled at her to get on and sit down. That's why she won't talk to anyone now."

"Hollis," Leta said, "That reminds me—Algie's having nightmares about Oscar. That was what I was going to tell you earlier."

Hollis frowned. "He told me his nightmares were about the water."

"He has nightmares about getting grabbed, too. He told me so. And . . . " She stopped.

Hollis frowned. "What?"

"Last night, he wet the bed."

Hollis stared. "You're kidding."

Leta shook her head. "I had to help him clean it up. We tried to be quiet."

Dray snorted. "Not that quiet. You woke me up. I felt bad for the little guy. He and Lolo seem to be stressin' the hardest."

Hollis glanced at Algie, who sat, as always, watching TV with his gnome.

"I don't know what to do with him," Leta said. "I hope we find Gee soon. I mean," she continued, "I have nightmares, too. About those explosions on the levee. And then the water hitting the house. I want them to go away. They're awful." With a shiver, she turned back to Kiki. "Does Maleeki live with y'all?"

"Yeah," she said. "He got taken away from his mother, because she didn't have any food in the house and was never home."

"You ever live with your dad?" Hollis asked Maleeki.

Maleeki stared at him in astonished rage and clenched his fists. "Get lost." He spun around and stalked off to his cot.

"His parents were never really together," Kiki said. "I don't think he's met his dad, and now his mom is in jail for I-don't-even-know-what. We don't talk to Maleeki about his parents, 'cause it makes him mad."

Hollis gazed across the room at Maleeki, feeling more sympathetic toward him now that he knew what he'd been through. Up until then, Hollis had thought of Maleeki as being a big waste of everybody's time. When Maleeki turned his head and stared back at him, Hollis tried a grin. Maleeki's eyes narrowed, and his lip curled. As his expression sharpened into a glare, the dislike he felt for Hollis flew across the room and took away Hollis's grin. Hollis turned around, wondering what he'd done to make Maleeki so angry.

He's up to something. And I bet that something includes me.

Chapter 19

Rebound

Hollis tried to put Maleeki out of his mind. He decided to avoid the other boy for as long as possible. *No point in looking for trouble.* Since a new set of donations had arrived, he went to find Eden some dusting powder to replace the one she'd given him. On his way to the donation tables, however, he ran right into Maleeki.

"Hey," Maleeki said.

Hollis's eyes narrowed. "What?"

Maleeki showed his teeth in a semi-smile and waved his hand. "Lotsa people here, huh?"

Hollis nodded. "I guess."

"Know any of 'em before you got here?"

At first, Hollis thought about his conversation with Eden about his dad. He was about to answer when something in Maleeki's expression stopped him. *Oh no—he's onto me about Oscar.* "No."

"Me either. Kind of weird, don't cha think? So many people from the same town, and none of us know each other."

"A lot of people live in New Orleans."

"Heh, yeah, you right about that. Well, later." Maleeki strolled away.

Hollis watched him go. *Better warn Leta—Eden too.* He found Eden quickly and then looked for Leta.

"Hey, Leta, if anyone asks if we know Oscar, don't tell them, okay? I told Eden, and she says she won't say anything either."

"Why not?" she asked.

"Just do it," Hollis pleaded.

"Not until you say why."

With an exasperated sigh, Hollis quietly told her all about hiding Maleeki's loot on Oscar's cot. Since Hollis had always considered Leta a goody-two-shoes, her reaction surprised him.

"That was you?" she asked, admiration in her voice. "Too cool! I'm proud of you, Hollis. So Kiki was right about Maleeki stealing. It's stupid that he takes things from people—we've all lost so much. Don't worry. I'll tell him we don't know a soul."

Hollis nodded. *Good! He can't find out anything now.*

An hour later, he saw Maleeki watching Cartoon Network with Algie and Gnomie. He bit his lip. *Never thought of warning Algie. Gonna have to watch myself. Maleeki's gonna be out for blood now.* He sighed and left to wash up for the night.

Saturday opened to a beautiful day. After breakfast, the children's group played outside while Miss Violet watched them. Lolo ran to the large sandbox on one side of the play area. Algie followed her, dragging his feet and his gnome. Leta and the other girls took over the patio with their jump rope and soon were locked in a hot contest of Double Dutch.

Hollis turned his face toward the sun, reveling in the warmth after so much time indoors. Drayden and Maleeki walked past him, Dray bouncing a basketball.

"Hollis?" Dray held up the ball. "You play?"

Hollis nodded and followed them to the half-court.

"Y'all wanna play one on one?" Maleeki asked. "Or do we gotta use rules?"

"You mean 'one on one on one,'" Dray said, laughing.

Hollis grinned, but his attention left the court. Oscar had sauntered out of the shelter, peeped around, and scuttled into the street.

"Hang on, guys," Hollis told the other two. "I wanna get some water."

Since the fountain was near the gate, Hollis could see down the street as he bent over and slurped the water. He watched as Oscar met two other men. Their actions—the way they stood, the way their hands moved, and the way they glanced around to see if anyone was watching—said plenty. He'd seen drug deals go down in his neighborhood.

"Come on, Hollis," Dray hollered. "Let's go!"

Hollis ran back and the game was on.

Much to Hollis's annoyance, Maleeki turned out to be the best basketball player in the group. He was fast and tall, and he ran rings around Dray and Hollis.

"I win again!" Maleeki said at last. "Y'all slow. That was the easiest win yet."

"How 'bout you play me?" Eden asked, laying down her end of the jump-rope.

"I ain't playin' no girl," Maleeki scoffed.

"Scared?" Eden asked.

"No. Don't wanna embarrass you."

"I can take it if I lose," she said. "Can you?"

"I won't. All right, who's first?"

"You." She smiled. "I'll finish."

Maleeki rolled his eyes. "Whatever."

"C'mon, everybody," Calaya called to the other children. "Eden's gonna whup Maleeki at basketball."

The rest of the children stopped what they were doing and ran over to watch. Several of the adults who had come outside to smoke joined the crowd of onlookers.

"Wow," Leta said to Hollis as Eden dodged past Maleeki and tossed the ball into the basket. "Eden's good."

"She could beat me," he said, twisting his lips. "She got another one. That ties it up again, five to five. It's gonna be tight. Hope Eden wins."

"Me too." Leta hugged herself. "There sure are a lot of people out here now. Seems like half the shelter is in the yard."

"I bet they want Eden to win too," Hollis said with a grin.

"They would if they knew all the things Maleeki's been doing. Aw, Maleeki's ahead again!"

"Not for long," Hollis said, watching Eden slap the ball away.

Dribbling out of the back court, she took a step in one direction and

Maleeki leaped to block her. In a flash, she changed direction, shifting the ball to her other hand and tossing it through the net.

An "ahhh" rippled through the growing crowd.

"*Both hands!*" crowed Hollis. "Eden's a—a—"

"Ambidextrous," Leta said.

"Uh oh," Hollis said, covering his eyes with his hand.

Outcries and grumbles came from the watchers.

Kiki jumped forward and grabbed the ball away from Maleeki, who scowled at her.

"What happened?" Leta asked.

A man behind her said, "Boy threw an elbow. Hope the girl's all right."

"You okay, Eden?" Kiki asked.

Eden grinned and nodded.

"Do that again," Kiki snarled in her cousin's face, "and it'll be game over, Eden on top."

Maleeki shrugged and, taking the ball, walked to the back court.

Leta hunched her shoulders as a nearby adult jostled her. "It's getting too crowded. I hope they finish soon."

"They play to ten, and it's eight to eight now. He missed! Eden's ball."

"Oh man, Maleeki stole it. Figures, right Hollis?"

Hollis smiled at Leta's joke. "She's got it back. Needs two to win. Come on, Eden!"

Eden floated toward the net, her feet moving like a dancer's. Maleeki, with eyes darting and teeth clenched, shifted and bounced in front of her. Changing directions twice, Eden twisted past him and leaped into the air. The ball swished into the net for Eden's ninth point. As it fell through the net, Eden landed, caught the ball, and pitched it to Maleeki. Immediately stealing it away from him again, she shot from the far edge of the half-court. The ball bounced once, twice on the rim and toppled in.

The crowd roared.

"Oh, *man!*" Hollis screamed to Leta, who had her hands over her ears. "She got him!"

Leta rolled her eyes and nodded.

Hollis continued, "Maleeki'll never get over gettin' beat by a girl. In front of everyone in the shelter, too!"

As if to prove Hollis's point, Maleeki glared at everyone and stomped away.

As the crowd disbanded, Kiki appeared at Leta's shoulder with a frightened expression on her face. "I can't find Lolo. Anywhere."

Chapter 20

Red Beans

Leta frowned at Kiki and looked toward the sandbox. "But she and Algie were right over there."

"Where's Algie?" Hollis asked.

Leta shook her head. "They probably went to the bathroom. Let's go find Miss Violet."

Miss Violet was congratulating Eden. When she was told about the missing children, she called the rest of their group, and they clustered around her while she checked the yard. None of the others had seen the children either.

"Let's split up," Miss Violet said. "Kiki, Hollis, Leta, you come with me. Everyone else, keep searching the playground. If we can't find them, we'll have to get more people to help."

"Yes, ma'am," Calaya said.

As the children spread out to search the playground, Miss Violet hurried into the shelter with Hollis and the two girls.

"Let's check the bathrooms," Leta said. "I'll bet they're there."

But Lolo and Algie weren't in either of them.

"I don't see them in the main room anywhere," Miss Violet said, worry in her voice.

"What about the kitchen?" Hollis suggested. "Maybe they wanted a drink."

Kiki ran ahead to the kitchen door and checked inside. "Here they are," she yelled to the others. "They're with Mr. Red Beans."

Miss Violet frowned until she walked through the door and saw Red washing Lolo's tear-stained face at the sink. When Red saw Miss Violet and the children entering the kitchen, he looked up and grinned.

"Red," Miss Violet began in a warning tone.

"I know, I know, Violet," he said, nodding his head. "I should have brought them straight to you. But the little girl had somethin' in her eye, and she was cryin' so hard that all I thought about was helpin' her."

"She *said* she had something in her eye?" Kiki asked him.

Mr. Red shook his head. "She never said a word. The little boy told me, right Algie?"

Algie nodded. "L-Lolo got sand in her eye and r-ran away. I ran t-too so she wouldn't be by herself. Mr. Red Beans saw us and helped."

Hollis could see that Lolo's eye was bloodshot, and Leta asked Lolo if it still hurt. Lolo shook her head and smiled at Red, who pinched her cheek.

Nodding to Miss Violet, he said, "It'll never happen again, Violet. I'm not tryin' to cause no trouble."

She patted his shoulder and went out to collect the rest of the children.

The kids, including Maleeki, trailed into the shelter and gathered in the children's section. Lolo's disappearance had distracted them from Eden's triumph over Maleeki. No one seemed to feel like teasing him anymore. Miss Violet noticed the group's downcast mood and asked them what was wrong.

"Well," said Calaya. "Feels like all we have is each other, and then these two disappear."

Everyone nodded.

"When I couldn't find them," Kiki said, "it felt like the whole world was fallin' apart—again."

Eden nodded. "We've lost our families, our things, our neighbors."

"All the schools," Leta said.

"The basketball courts and playgrounds," said Dray.

"We don't know if our friends are okay," said Kiki.

"The whole city is gone," Eden finished, "And we can't find our families."

"You have me," Miss Violet reminded them.

Eden tried to smile, but her lips wobbled. "Thanks, Miss Violet," she said finally. "We know we can count on you. Thanks for helping us find them."

"I think we need to limit the time you all watch the news," Miss Violet said.

"But we want to know what's happening!" said Kiki.

While everyone else started arguing with Miss Violet about watching the news, Hollis sighed and wandered over to his bed. He didn't care if they could watch the news or not. Leta kept thinking they'd see Jonas, but Hollis didn't believe it would happen. He was afraid he'd never see either Gee or Jonas again.

Glancing down, he saw someone's shirt lying across his bed. When he picked it up, he saw a tiny, brown bottle underneath. A crack vial. He held it up and peered inside. Out of the corner of his eye, he saw Miss Violet's head turn. She stopped talking and walked over to him.

"Where did you get that, Hollis?" she asked, taking the bottle from him.

"It was here on my bed," he told her. "I swear, I've never seen it before."

"Are you *sure* it isn't yours?" she said.

Hollis nodded and backed away.

Miss Violet held the bottle up to the light. "There's something inside."

Hollis reached out to touch her arm. "I swear. It's not mine, Miss Violet."

She looked at him, her eyes filled with sympathy. "I believe you, Hollis, but this is the kind of bottle that people keep drugs in. There are rules I have to follow for this sort of thing. I'm afraid we're going to have to call the police."

Chapter 21

Lolo and the Po-Po

"Appears to be cocaine. Have to test it, though," said Officer Bradford, peering with one eye into the bottle. He rocked back and forth on his heels, his belly hanging over his belt. Officer O'Neil, a thin and short blond, nodded and squinted at the bottle from over his partner's shoulder. One of them reeked of Old Spice, and Hollis gagged.

"You *sure* you've never seen this before?" Officer Bradford asked Hollis.

Hollis shook his head.

"They're starting younger and younger these days," the officer said to Miss Violet.

"But I've never used a drug in my life!" Hollis said. "Test me."

Officer Bradford eyed Hollis with suspicion. "Might just do that," he said. He tossed the bottle up and caught it. "We're going out to the unit to test this." He glared at Hollis. "Then we'll decide if we're going to test *you*."

"Back soon," Officer O'Neil said as they left. "And don't try to go anywhere."

Dropping down on his cot, Hollis put his chin in his hands. He couldn't believe this was happening. Miss Violet patted his shoulder but stopped and turned to see Lolo tugging at her skirt.

"What is it, Lolo?" Miss Violet asked her. Lolo pointed at Hollis. "Yes, that's Hollis," she said.

Lolo tugged on her skirt again and pointed at Hollis. Miss Violet sighed, her face sagging more than usual. "Does anyone know what she's trying to say?"

Algie stood up and pointed to Hollis. "Hollis, Lolo? Hollis?"

Lolo shook her head and walked over, still pointing.

Algie joined her. "B-Bed?" he asked, patting the cot.

Lolo nodded, her eyes sparkling.

Miss Violet took over the questioning. "Did you see something, Lolo? Did you see someone put the bottle on Hollis's bed?"

Lolo nodded again and clapped her hands.

Hope soared in Hollis's chest. By this time, everyone's eyes were fixed on Lolo.

"Who, Lolo? Who did you see?" Miss Violet asked.

Lolo spun around and darted out of the children's corner. Miss Violet tried to catch her, but Lolo slipped out of reach and ran toward the adult section of the shelter. The entire group scrambled to catch the little girl, but she eluded everyone. She led them straight to Oscar, lying on his cot and filling out some paperwork for financial aid. When Miss Violet and the other children caught up to the little girl, Lolo pointed at Oscar, who looked up and returned Miss Violet's stare.

With a sigh, Miss Violet asked, "Oscar, did you put something on Hollis's cot?"

Hollis put the pieces together. *Of course he did! I should have known when I saw the shirt. Bet Maleeki told him I put the stolen stuff on his cot. His revenge wasn't too smart though, using drugs. Now the police are here. When they search him, it'll be game over!*

Oscar rose, keeping his eyes on Miss Violet. *He looks kind of sick. Desperate.* Knowing what happened at the parking lot, Hollis reached for Lolo's shoulder to pull her away, but Oscar grabbed her first.

Miss Violet threw up her hands, as if to tell Oscar to stop. He didn't pay notice. An open penknife appeared in his hand, and he clutched Lolo closer, the knife pressed against her neck.

"Gonna get my stuff and leave," he snarled at Miss Violet. "Before them cops come back."

Hollis scanned the room. No one had been looking when Oscar grabbed Lolo, and no one realized the danger he posed. Everyone was either outside watching the police or inside watching the police through the windows.

Miss Violet nodded, her face pale and her hands clenched. "Give Lolo to me, and you can leave."

Oscar shook his head. "I'll let her go outside." He looked at Hollis. "I kep' my word with your brother, didn't I, kid?"

Hollis nodded.

"I kep' my word then, and I'll keep it now. I'll give her to you outside, but I'm not goin' out that front door. The po-po are there. There's other doors outta here, but they're all locked. You got keys, I know."

Miss Violet took a breath, but Hollis never found out what she was going to say. Lolo, a furious expression on her face, opened her mouth and howled, "Mr. Red Beans! Help! Help!"

"Huh? Lolo?" Mr. Red's voice came from the far left side of the room.

Hollis spotted the big man as he turned from the window, his head twisting right and left. When Red locked eyes with him, Hollis jerked his head. Red bounded toward them.

"I'm comin', baby girl!" he yelled.

People in his path jumped aside as his heavy footsteps headed their way. Oscar whirled around to confront him. Red stopped an arm's length away, and the two men eyed one another. Everyone in the shelter knew what was happening now. Hollis wished someone would signal the police, but everyone was too intent on watching the scene to think of calling for help. The murmur of whispered questions faded into silence.

"Whatcha doin', Oscar?" Mr. Red Beans asked in a pleasant voice, as though he were asking him how his day was going.

"I'm leavin'," Oscar snapped. "You stay outta this, Red!" He blinked.

For a big man, Mr. Red Beans sure was fast. He struck the moment Oscar's eyes were closed. His hand lashed out and grabbed Oscar's arm, and he yanked the knife away from Lolo's neck. With his other hand, he swept the child away from Oscar and tucked her safely under his own arm. Oscar staggered for a moment in surprise, still holding the tiny knife. Seconds later, that was in Red's hands, too.

"Get those police fellas, Violet," Mr. Red said.

Miss Violet scurried toward the front doors. When she returned with the police, Officer Bradford snapped the cuffs on Oscar, and several of the evacuees patted Red on his back and shoulder. "You a hero, Beans," Mrs. Wiley said and kissed his cheek.

"I'm sorry I didn't listen to you, Hollis," Miss Violet told him. "You were right—he was dangerous. We should have kicked him out before." Hollis smiled.

Mr. Red Beans knelt in front of Lolo. "That you who called me?" She nodded.

"Thought so. Now, anyone that can yell that loud can say 'thank you' to me in her own voice. You not goin' back to not talkin'."

Lolo threw her arms around the big man's neck. "Thank you very much," she said. Mr. Red hugged her and then turned her over to Kiki, who hugged her too.

"Lolo, Lolo," Kiki said. "You're a hero, too! I can't believe you were so brave. You saved Hollis!"

Hollis stepped up for his hug. "Thank you, Lolo," he said solemnly. Lolo stuck her finger in her mouth and grinned at him.

Chapter 22

The Right Thing

Several days passed. Nothing new came to light about the location of any of the families.

"I'm sorry, children," Miss Violet kept saying. "These things take time."

"A week. We've been here a whole week," Hollis grumbled to Leta. "Where's Algie?"

"Watching Cartoon Network with Gnomie. What else? He never eats breakfast anymore."

"The only thing he likes here is donuts. I don't think missing those is gonna kill him. He still wetting the bed?"

Leta nodded. "Wakes up sweating and crying every night. Every morning, he's wet. And every night, you sleep right through it."

Hollis gnawed on his upper lip. "Sorry. Guess I have my own bad dreams. Hopefully, this'll all stop when we find Gee."

"*If* we find her," Leta muttered.

"Don't say that, Leta—we agreed. Gee is alive, and we're not gonna talk like she ain't."

"Sorry," Leta said. "I get scared." She looked toward the TV. "I think I'll tell Algie Gnomie wants him to eat breakfast."

Hollis sighed. It felt weird depending on a polyresin lawn ornament.

After breakfast, Hollis wandered back to his cot. He had slept okay the night before, but he still felt tired. Dropping onto his cot, he decided a nap would help him get through this miserable anniversary.

"Hollis, I need your help." Eden's voice interrupted him as he nodded off. He opened one eye. "Somethin's wrong with Maleeki."

Hollis closed the eye. "You're not tellin' me anything I don't already know."

"I'm serious. He's not himself. He won't talk to anyone, not even Kiki or Lolo. He won't eat or go outside with us. He doesn't even sleep on his cot."

Hollis opened his eye again. "Where's he sleepin'?"

Eden shook her head. "I have no idea."

He rolled over. "What do you want, Eden?"

"I want you to talk to him."

"He's not gonna talk to me. He hates me. Get Kiki. She's family."

"She tried. We've all tried. You think I'd ask you first? You're the last one I came to."

Hollis sat up. "Who cares if he's not around? All that means is that we get to hang onto our stuff a little longer. I can't believe we still have the Game Boys those Episcopalians gave us."

Eden scowled. "I know he's a pain. But if we don't take care of each other, who will?"

"You're not my mama, Eden, and you're not his. It'd be better if you stopped gettin' in everybody's business and just relaxed. That's what I'm gonna do." He lay back once more.

"Well, gee, Hollis. Seems all you think about is yourself! We all lived through that hurricane, you know."

Hollis rolled onto his stomach and made a big show of snuggling his face into his pillow. He heard Eden's foot scrape the floor as she turned again to go, and he waited with bated breath. No footsteps. He sighed.

Sure enough, her voice came again. "Hollis. You talk a lot about finding your father. What if he's like Maleeki? Or Oscar? Or in jail like Maleeki's mama? How you gonna feel then? Might need someone to talk to. What if there isn't anyone 'cause everyone left you?"

Hollis stayed quiet. Eden stomped her foot and gave a frustrated growl. At last, Hollis heard footsteps walking away.

He sat up and rubbed his face. *Who could sleep after that?* Eden's comment about everyone leaving him cut awfully close to the bone. *Maleeki acts like a jerk, and I'm the bad guy.* He got out of bed. *She's got a point, though. I want to find my dad, not be him.*

Maleeki was outside. Hollis saw him from a window. Cutting through the kitchen, he slipped out of a back door while one of the cooks was taking out the trash.

A scowl greeted Hollis as he approached. Maleeki pulled up a handful of grass and flicked it at him.

Glad there aren't any rocks out here. Hollis sat down.

"Go away," Maleeki snarled.

"Glad to," Hollis said. "Once I get what I want. I don't want Eden sweatin' me anymore, Maleeki, so I've gotta find out what's going on with you. Then she'll leave me alone."

"Well, you outta luck. I'm not tellin' you nothin'. You can leave me alone."

"Then talk to Kiki."

"Get lost."

Hollis frowned. "I'm not leaving until you talk to me or Kiki. Wherever you go, I'll go. I've followed you before. You know it. I'll drive you crazy 'til you tell someone what's wrong."

Maleeki's head sagged. A big tear slid down his nose and fell into the grass.

"You can go tell them I'm cryin'," Maleeki said. "Then y'all can all laugh at me."

Hollis recoiled. "Are you nuts? Those are *girls* in there. I go tell them you're cryin', and they'll be out here in two seconds, crawlin' all over us. It'll be a nightmare. They'll never let me alone."

"Why won't they leave *you* alone?"

"Because they'll want to know what I did to make you cry, and I can't tell them, because I don't know."

Maleeki sniffled.

"My life won't be worth living. They'll follow me everywhere. There'll be nowhere to hide."

"Like you were gonna do to me," Maleeki said, glaring.

"Exactly. So I'm not gonna call them out here."

"Why not? I like the idea of the girls drivin' you crazy."

"Yeah, but they won't just do it to me. They'll do it to you, too. They'll

drive both of us insane. C'mon, Maleeki! We're in this together now."
Hollis changed tactics. "Eden said she tried everything. If I can't get it
out of you, they'll think they're out of options. You'll be just as doomed
as me. I mean, are you missing your aunt and uncle or something? Just
tell me!"

Maleeki shook his head. "Nah, they're too strict. I'm always in trouble
with them. I miss my real mom, but I'm kinda used to that."

"How long has she been in jail—I mean, away?"

"Couple of years."

Hollis felt his patience sliding away again. "So what is it then?"

Maleeki glared at him.

He's never gonna talk. I'm wasting my time. Hollis started to fidget as
he stared back at Maleeki.

"It's Lolo," Maleeki said.

Hollis was confused. "What about her?"

"It was my fault that guy took her."

"Your fault? How?"

"I told him you put that stuff on his bed. I didn't know he'd hurt
Lolo, though."

"Just me," Hollis said.

"You deserved it. I had to get you back for stealin' my stuff."

"I didn't steal your stuff. It was stuff you stole."

"Yeah, but once I stole it, it was mine. You took it. That's stealin'."

Hollis rolled his eyes. Maleeki was hopeless. "How'd you find out it
was me? Algie?"

"Yeah. How'd you guess?"

"I saw you talking. I'd warned Leta. Never thought about Algie."
Hollis leaned back. "That was pretty good, Maleeki. You're like a real
detective."

Maleeki puffed out his chest.

"So what you want to do now?" Hollis went on.

Maleeki's scowl returned. "I'm not tellin' them what I did. I'm only
tellin' you, because . . . well, I don't know why I'm tellin' you. But I'm
not tellin' them."

"Why not? They already know you steal. You didn't mean for the man to go after Lolo. Go apologize. They'll forgive you."

Maleeki lowered his chin. "No!" he yelled.

"Why?" Hollis yelled back.

"Because they'll hate me!" Maleeki screamed.

Hollis dropped his voice back to normal. "No, they won't. They'll like you, because you admitted what you did. If you don't tell them, you're gonna keep moping, and they're gonna keep buggin' you. If I were you, I'd just do it."

Standing up, Hollis extended his hand to Maleeki. Maleeki scowled, but he let Hollis pull him to his feet. Together, they went inside to find everyone else.

When Maleeki told his story, they all praised him for being honest. Hollis left as they began patting Maleeki on the back. *I guess for Maleeki, being honest at all is a big deal.*

Maleeki started talking to Kiki and Lolo again and ignoring everyone else, who seemed fine with that. Happy that Hollis had gotten Maleeki to return to the group, Eden was being extra nice to him.

The next morning, Leta strolled over and plopped down on Hollis's cot. "Y'know, Hollis, this place isn't so bad. I'll be glad when we find Jonas and Gee, but I'll be sad to leave here. Is that wrong?"

Hollis shook his head. "I know what you mean. I'll miss them all, too. Even Miss Violet."

Leta sighed in relief. "Yeah. But Algie is having such a hard time. I'm worried about him. He's gotten so quiet. All he does is watch TV, sleep, and drag that stupid gnome around. He isn't even hanging with Lolo anymore."

Hollis frowned. "I don't know what to do. We just have to find Gee—she would make him all right." He paused. "Leta, I've been thinking. D'you think Dad is like Oscar or Maleeki?"

Leta bit her lip. "I never thought of that. Yeah, he could be. It seems like he's one of those people who don't do the right thing."

"We don't know if he's *still* like that."

"Sure we do," Leta said. "He's not here." She went off to play with the other girls.

Lying back on his cot, Hollis closed his eyes but found it hard to close his thoughts, too.

What if Dad is in jail like Oscar or Maleeki's mom? Do I really want to find him if that's how he is? He rolled on his cot. He wasn't so relaxed after all.

Chapter 23

Hard Heads

Two days later, Eden approached Hollis again. He was sitting alone under a tree when she found him, and he watched as she came toward him.

Maleeki again.

"Hey, Hollis?" she said, appearing unsure of her welcome.

"Yeah, Eden?"

"Well, Maleeki . . ."

I knew it! "No way, Eden. I'm done."

"But last time you got him to come clean!" She waved her hand, and Kiki trotted across the playground to join them. "Just let me tell you what it is. It's important, I swear."

"No!" Hollis said, feeling like they were ganging up on him.

"The Wiley brothers are missing their Game Boys. Mrs. Wiley is going to call the police."

"Good!" Hollis snapped. "He needs to get arrested."

"But Hollis," Kiki pleaded, "what if he gets stuck in jail here and can't go home when Mom and Dad find us?"

"They'll probably throw a party," Hollis grumbled.

"No, they won't. We took Maleeki in because his parents weren't any good and we wanted to help. No matter how bad he acted, we always knew he could change."

"Well, he ain't gonna change," Hollis shot back. "People don't change unless they want to, and Maleeki don't want to. Besides," he said, glancing at the court where Maleeki was shooting baskets, "my Dad did wrong, and I turned out okay."

Kiki said something else, but Hollis stopped listening. *I've changed. I don't want to find him anymore. He don't deserve it.* Looking up, he realized the two girls were staring at him.

"You okay?" Eden asked.

Hollis pulled himself together and stood up. Nodding at Kiki, he said, "I didn't hear you."

"I said, you can't throw someone out of your family just because they're jerks. I thought you'd understand that more than anyone, Hollis."

"Not anymore," Hollis said. Noticing Kiki's distressed face, he sighed. *I don't like Kiki being upset. She really is like family.* "Fine. I'll take care of it. For *you,* Kiki."

She clapped her hands and hugged him. "Thanks, Hollis," she said over her shoulder as she skipped away.

Hollis turned to Eden. "I'm gonna do what you want. Now go on with Kiki."

"What're you going to do?" she asked.

"Eden," he said, staring her in the eye, "I said I'd take care of it. You don't need to worry how. I'll let you know when it's done."

Looking both impressed and uncertain, she went off to huddle with Kiki and Calaya, who sat watching Maleeki outshoot Dray. Hollis, feeling out of his depth, decided he needed bigger guns to help with this assignment.

An hour later, Hollis was back under a donation table. *These things sure are handy.* He peered out of the gap between the tablecloths but ducked when Maleeki approached, escorted by Mr. Red Beans.

"Come over here," said Mr. Red Beans. "There's somethin' you'll like on this table, Maleeki, I promise you."

"What is it?" Hollis heard Maleeki say. Footsteps shuffled closer.

"It's the opportunity not to go to jail," Mr. Red Beans said.

"Huh?" Maleeki sounded startled.

"I want the Wileys' Game Boys back."

"I don't have them."

"You do."

"I don't."

"I know that you do."

After a short silence, Maleeki asked, "How do you know?"

Hah! Hollis thought. *Gotcha.*

"Someone saw you."

"Hollis!" Maleeki growled.

"Hollis? No. Hollis has other things to do. You don't know who it is, trust me. But they know you. And if you don't get those Game Boys, I'm goin' over to where you sleep, and I'm gonna go through everything until I find them."

Hollis pictured the towering size of Mr. Red Beans. He didn't think Maleeki would argue.

"He's gone to get them, Hollis," Mr. Red whispered.

"Thanks, Mr. Red Beans."

"No problem, boy. Anytime, I told you. Here he comes." After a pause, Hollis heard him say, "That's good, Maleeki. Now. Listen carefully." Hollis found himself leaning forward to listen, too. "If I ever hear of you stealin' again, I'll—" Mr Red Beans stopped.

"You'll what?" Maleeki asked, sounding scared.

"I'll make you give back what you took again. I'm not gonna hit you, boy, or yell. I'm just tryin' to keep you out of trouble. Think you could help me with that?"

"I'll try," Maleeki mumbled.

"Well, I appreciate that. Now you go on and have a blessed day."

Hollis heard Maleeki run off.

"Hollis?" Mr. Red Beans called. "You want me to give them back to the Wileys for you?"

"Yeah. That would be perfect. Thanks again for your help." He thought for a moment. Still under the table, he said, "Mr. Red Beans?"

"Yeah?"

"You got any kids?"

"Nah. I work with them though. I teach first grade."

"You got to get your own. You'd be a really good dad."

"Why, thanks." Red paused. "Hollis, you sound sad. Your dad not who he needs to be?"

Hollis hesitated before answering. "No."

"Don't give up, boy. Life has a way of makin' a man wake up."

"Like Oscar?"

"Well, that's a good point. Maybe what happened here will make Oscar think. You're right, though; some people never learn. I did. I stopped runnin' the streets, went back to school, and now I'm a teacher. I've never been happier."

"What made *you* stop?"

"Well, Hollis, I . . . " Mr. Red Beans cleared his throat, paused, and cleared it again.

"That's okay. You don't have to tell me. It's none of my business anyway. I just wondered what kind of thing has to happen before people change who they are."

"It has to be somethin' big." He paused. "For me, it was nearly gettin' myself shot."

Under the table, Hollis's eyes widened. "Really?"

Red Beans sighed. "I haven't thought about it in a long time. I was somewhere I had no business being, and the guy I was trying to get something from decided to rob me instead. I snatched his gun out of his hand, but it went off, grazing my head. I've still got a scar where no hair'll grow. When I got home, I decided that my life needed a new direction."

"Feels weird for me to hope that my dad gets shot."

"Maybe it don't have to be that drastic. Anyway, I'm gonna go find Mrs. Wiley before she calls the police. Remember, Hollis, you can't control much in this world."

Katrina taught me that.

Hollis heard Mr. Red Beans's footsteps fading away. Crawling to the end of the table, Hollis sneaked out from under the tablecloth and went to give Eden the report that his job was completed.

"What did you do?" Eden asked.

Hollis walked away, smiling.

"Hollis!" Eden called out. "Tell me what you did. C'mon!"

Shaking his head stubbornly, Hollis went back to his cot and thought about everything that had happened. Leta was right. He'd miss it here. He even wished he could take his cot home. He'd done so much changing and growing and thinking on it that he'd become quite attached to it.

But now he had a decision to make about his father. Asking Gee to find him would upset her a lot. He'd always known that, but for the first time, he realized why. He wanted her to know that he understood now. He knew he'd been wrong about Gee and his mother being the reason his father left. As these thoughts tumbled through his head, he drifted off to sleep in a well-deserved nap.

Chapter 24

Katrina's Kids

On Friday, twelve days after Katrina hit New Orleans, Hollis woke up to find the shelter aflutter with excitement. With the news that a television crew was on its way to the shelter to conduct interviews, everyone was in a high state of anticipation. Everyone, that is, but Algie.

"He's gettin' worse and worse, isn't he?" Dray asked Hollis after Algie picked up Gnomie and announced that he hated everyone.

Hollis sighed. "We been here too long for Algie."

"We been here too long for me. Nothin' we can do about it, though. I guess he's still too young to get it. Where's Lolo? She usually cheers him up."

Hollis nodded. "She does, but the 'Lolo maneuver' hasn't worked lately. She's tired of being here, too." He pointed to Lolo, who was leaning against Kiki with a mulish expression on her face.

Shaking their heads, Hollis and Dray went to eat a late breakfast. The only person still in the dining area was Maleeki. When Dray sat down across from him, Hollis sat on Dray's other side and wished he'd been the one to choose the table. It wouldn't have been anywhere near Maleeki.

Maleeki scowled and pointed his fork at Hollis as he sat down. "You ratted me out to Mr. Red Beans."

Dray's eyes slid from Maleeki to Hollis and back again.

"I don't know what you're talking about," Hollis said through a mouthful of egg. He avoided Maleeki's eye.

Maleeki snorted. "Stop followin' me around and pay attention to your brother."

Hollis looked up defiantly. "I can take care of Algie."

"Oh yeah?" Maleeki asked. "I see he's not at breakfast. As usual."

"He doesn't have to eat breakfast." Hollis continued to shovel eggs into his mouth.

"What about lunch? He says he's not gonna eat lunch either."

"He'll eat lunch. I'll see to it."

"Oh yeah?" Maleeki's voice squeaked in glee. "You haven't been."

"Whaddaya mean?" Hollis asked, irritated.

Maleeki smiled. "Algie hasn't eaten since he got here."

"That's impossible. It's almost been two weeks."

"I know," Maleeki said. "You didn't notice. You were too busy bein' all over me like you are."

Hollis narrowed his eyes. "If that's true, how did *you* find out about it?"

"Algie told me. Miss Violet found a sweet potato pie she was gonna buy for him. He told her no. I asked him why. He said he wasn't gonna eat until they found his grandmother." Maleeki picked up his tray, cocked an eyebrow at Hollis, and left the dining room.

Dray sat forward. "Huh. Think he's lyin'?"

"I hope so." Leaving his breakfast behind, Hollis went to find Algie.

"Why's everyone s-so excited?" Algie asked Leta as Hollis joined them.

"There are TV people are coming to interview us," Leta said.

Hollis surveyed Algie from his curly head to his Spongebob tennis shoes. He *did* seem thinner. Maybe a lot thinner. Part of the problem was that Algie took new clothes out of donations every day. Since he always picked oversized, baggy shirts and pants that Gee would never have let him wear, his actual size was hard to see. Hollis decided to talk to Leta before he confronted Algie.

"I d-don't want to be inter—inter—I d-don't want to be on TV!" Algie announced. "I want Gee!"

"We do too, Algie," Leta said, trying to hug him. He pulled away and lay down on his cot, tucking his face into Gnomie's hard beard.

Hollis jerked his head for Leta to follow him into the hallway. Out of

Algie's earshot, Hollis explained. "Maleeki says Algie hasn't eaten since he's been here. Is that even possible?"

Leta covered her mouth with her hands and nodded. "It could be! He's always either tearing up his food or taking it off somewhere. And he's been losing weight. I thought it was just because he wasn't eating breakfast, but . . . That little brat!"

Hollis drew in a deep breath. "Go get him."

Leta scuttled off and returned with a scowling Algie in tow.

"He says he's not eating until we find Gee," Leta said.

"You will so," Hollis said.

Algie glared.

"If you don't eat, you'll get sick. If you get sick, you'll have to go to the hospital. If you go to the hospital and we find Gee, we won't be able to leave right away 'cause *you'll* be in the hospital. And what do you think Gee'd say? She's gonna be mad."

Algie shook his head. "I don't care what you say. I'm n-not s-sick. I f-feel good. And I'm n-not gonna eat *nothin'*."

"Just when do you feel good?" Leta asked. "You sleep all day, you have no energy, and you're crabby all the time. If you're not sick now, you will be soon."

Algie folded his arms and glared at her.

Hollis lectured, threatened, and reasoned with his brother for another half hour before he gave up. He watched Algie stomp away. *It was nice being the hero to make Maleeki 'fess up. But with Algie, I'm always the bad guy. How can I get him to understand?*

"We need to find Gee or Jonas fast," he told Leta. "We can't let Algie just starve himself to death."

"Think he'll keep refusing to eat?" she asked.

Hollis nodded. "Algie? Yeah, I do."

"Shouldn't we tell Miss Violet?"

Hollis thought for a moment. "Let's try to get him to eat today. We'll tell her tomorrow if he keeps saying no."

Although Leta and Hollis no longer cared, the excitement in the shelter continued to grow. Women lined up for Calaya to fix their hair, and a crowd formed around the donation tables as people searched for new outfits.

"Finally, somethin' fun to do," Hollis heard one woman say.

"Yeah," said another. "It's been awful borin'."

The CNN crew arrived with their lights, cameras, cords, and microphones, along with a silver-haired man named Harry Hathaway in a tight black T-shirt and jeans. Miss Violet gave the men a brief tour. After she told Harry Hathaway about the shelter, the lights came on, the cameras whirred, and the crew taped Hathaway telling the world about the state of New Orleans's refugees. He told Miss Violet that the segment would run at five that evening, when Alex Payne's show aired.

After recording Hathaway's conversation with Alex Payne, the crew filmed the evacuees eating lunch, the adults going outside to smoke, two men playing cards, and two others playing chess. Their cameras caught Calaya braiding Mrs. Wiley's hair and one of the families reading their Bible.

Near the end of the shoot, Harry Hathaway noticed the children's area. As Hollis watched, Hathaway pointed out the area to Miss Violet, and the two of them walked toward it.

". . . children here without their families," Miss Violet was saying as they reached Hollis's cot. "We're trying to locate them, but we haven't had much luck so far."

"That's terrible," Mr. Hathaway said, surveying the children sadly. "Thank you for letting us film here, Violet." He shook Miss Violet's hand.

As Mr. Hathaway turned to walk back toward the front of the shelter, Hollis jumped up from his cot. An idea dangled in front of him, and he grabbed it like a drowning man. "Excuse me," he said, waving at Mr. Hathaway.

The newscaster raised an eyebrow.

Hollis cleared his throat. "Do you think you could take a video of *us* and put it on TV? Our families might see us, and then we'll get found and you'll be a hero."

Harry Hathaway frowned. "Well," he said after a moment, "that's a really good idea. Let me see what I can do." He hurried off to get his crew.

Once the cameras were set up again, the crew filmed all of the children playing in the yard—all except for Algie, who still refused. After the shoot, they went inside so that Mr. Hathaway could wrap up the segment. While the crew gathered the children around Mr. Hathaway, Hollis sneaked a peek at the monitor and saw that the camera was zoomed in on Harry Hathaway's face.

"Yes, Alex," he said. "Katrina devastated New Orleans, but perhaps the most distressing thing I've seen is the children who have lost the ones they love the most."

Kiki poked Hollis in the side. "He means us," she said.

Hollis rolled his eyes.

"The ones who were supposed to take care of them, who just couldn't hang on in that terrible wind."

When Hollis glanced over at Kiki, he saw tears on her cheeks. Tears jumped into his eyes as well. He swiped a hand across his face.

"They were scattered to the farthest ends of the country," Mr. Hathaway continued. "We've seen them in Atlanta, in Houston, and in Memphis. Children caring for other children, lost in an inconceivable monster. Storm Children or, if you will, Katrina's Kids."

Hollis watched the monitor as the camera pulled back to show the children clustered around Mr. Hathaway. Into this warm picture of unity entered a seething little Fury—Algie, dragging Gnomie by his hat. Hollis froze, but his jaw dropped as he watched Algie march up to the CNN newscaster.

"We *ain't* Katrina's kids, mister," Algie yelled. "We're Gee Gaudet's kids." He swung Gnomie, whose pointed red hat right landed between Harry Hathaway's legs.

Hollis tore his eyes from the monitor and got himself moving, sprinting to grab his brother and pull him back. He apologized to Mr. Hathaway as the man moaned and sank into a squat. Mr. Hathaway waved his hand and forced a grin.

"Yes, yes, Alex," he wheezed through gritted teeth. "Apparently, I said the wrong thing." He tried to pat a glaring Algie on the head, but Algie ducked away. Hollis held him tight. Harry Hathaway laughed, allowing his hand to drop. "Cute little boy. Gee Gaudet, wherever you are, come get your child—for all our sakes. I'm Harry Hathaway for CNN."

Everyone laughed as the lights went off. Algie tried to retrieve Gnomie, who had fallen from his arms when Hollis grabbed him, but Hollis pulled him several feet back and held him fast.

The cameraman walked up to Harry Hathaway. "We can edit that out if you want."

Hathaway shook his head and bounced up and down in his squat, grunting. Finally, he straightened, picked up Algie's garden gnome, and strolled a bit crookedly over to Hollis and Algie. Squatting down in front of the little boy, he handed him the gnome. Algie clutched Gnomie to his chest.

"I hope your mother sees the segment."

Hollis gave Algie's arm a shake. Algie frowned. "Our m-mama's dead. Gee's our grandmother."

"Oh, I'm sorry," Mr. Hathaway said. "I didn't know. I hope you find her."

Algie nodded. "Sorry we hit you."

Mr. Hathaway grinned. "Actually, it was good. That little routine will get us both—" he glanced at Gnomie, "—er, *all* noticed. The network'll play it over and over. I ought to thank you two for doing it."

Algie cocked his head. "Want us to do it again?"

Chapter 25

Critical Conditions

Miss Violet sat in the children's corner, a smile on her face. "I have something to tell you all," she said. "I just found a Web site called the National Center for Missing and Exploited Children, where pictures of missing New Orleans children are being posted. It gives us another way to get your faces out to the public. Isn't that great?"

The children nodded. "Sounds terrific, Miss Violet," Kiki said.

"They've been around for a long time," Miss Violet went on, "but I only just found them today. As most of you know, I'm learning about all of this as I go on, and I just want to say that I'm sorry I didn't find it sooner."

"That's okay, Miss Violet," Kiki said. "We know you're trying."

"Well, we just have to get one of those digital cameras, and you'll be online for your families to find in no time."

"Miss Violet?" a volunteer called from across the room. "Telephone! They say it's urgent. I think it's about one of the kids."

Miss Violet scurried over and took the phone. A few minutes later, she placed her hand over the receiver and said, "Hollis? It's for you."

Everyone scrambled to their feet. Hollis and Leta looked at each other, Hollis hesitating.

"Go on!" Leta said, urging him with a wave of her arms.

"What if . . . " Hollis began, his heart pounding. "What if it's bad news?"

"It's news!" Eden said. "Go!"

Dragging his feet, Hollis crossed the room and took the receiver with a shaking hand.

Kiki and Calaya both skittered across to Leta, huddling with her and grabbing her hands. Everyone stared as Hollis spoke for a short time and handed the phone back to Miss Violet. He turned and trudged back toward the waiting group.

"He doesn't look happy," Leta said. "Oh no—Hollis! What's going on?"

Hollis looked at the floor. "Gee's in a coma."

As the children sat in a circle, Hollis was reminded of the day he, Leta, and Algie had joined the group. Of course, the conversation now was completely different.

"What's a c-coma?" Algie asked.

Leta hugged him. "It means Gee's in the hospital and can't wake up."

"So your grandmama's in Memphis? Did you talk to her doctor?" Eden asked.

Hollis shook his head. "I talked to the Jacksons, the man and woman she was rescued with. They had Jonas on threeway, so I talked to him too, but only for a minute. I didn't even get a chance to ask him what happened. He's in Houston at the Astrodome. We're all gonna meet up in Memphis."

"Wish I could talk to someone in *my* family," Dray said.

"When are you going?" Kiki asked.

"They said tomorrow," Hollis said.

Kiki sniffled. "Well, that's great!" A tear trickled down her cheek.

"Yeah," Calaya said in a wobbly voice. "We're so happy for you." She gulped and gave a tearful snort.

"I don't see why everybody is so upset," Maleeki said. "I can't wait 'til they get outta here."

"Shut up, Maleeki," Eden said.

"I can't believe it's all happening so fast," said Leta. "They'll find your families soon! And it'll be just like this for you!"

"I'll miss you." Calaya said, sniffling. "It's like I'm losin' part of my family again." She put her arm around Leta, who leaned against her. Kiki joined them.

Hollis nodded, his throat tight. He looked at Leta in a knot of hugs with Calaya and Kiki.

Leta's gonna miss all the girly stuff they do here—the hair, the nails, the gossip. Gee never has time for that. I hope she can keep in touch with Kiki and Calaya. I've never seen her so happy, all things considered.

"Miss Violet gave us the phone number here, so we can call," he said, his voice cracking even though he had cleared his throat.

"Can we take Lolo with us?" Algie asked, clutching his gnome.

"No, Algie," Hollis said with a smile. "I'd like to take them all with us, too. But Miss Violet says that they'll find Lolo's family soon."

Eden nodded and gave Hollis a hug. "I'll miss you most of all. Don't forget me."

Tears kept him from replying, but he knew he'd never forget. He didn't want to lose touch with Eden, either. Without knowing it, she had helped him change the most.

They sat a while longer, trying to think of other things to say. Finally, Miss Violet came to take them outside. None of them talked about it anymore, but they were subdued and stayed close together until it was time for bed.

The next morning, Hollis, Leta, and Algie hugged everyone goodbye again before climbing into a cab with Miss Violet. When the cab turned onto the highway and Hollis could no longer see the others waving to him, he, Leta, and Algie turned around in their seats.

"It was good to talk to Jonas last night," said Leta. "Thank goodness he's not dead. Don't have to worry about anyone anymore!"

Hollis sighed. "About Jonas, at least. Gee's still unconscious."

Leta nodded.

And I still haven't figured out what to say to Gee about Dad.

Chapter 26

Right Direction

⌒

Hollis peeled his forehead off the airplane's window, and Leta replaced it with hers as she leaned across his chest to see out.

"Do you see the airport?" she asked. "Is that Memphis? The pilot says we're landin' soon." She turned. "That means it's almost over, Algie." He sat next to her in the aisle seat holding Gnomie. "So are you gonna eat now?"

"W-when I see Gee," Algie declared, his eyebrows scrunched together and his eyes fierce. He lay his cheek against the gnome's red cone hat. "I d-don't like this r-ride. I d-didn't like the helichopper basket, and I d-don't like this. I'm n-never gonna f-fly again."

"C'mon, Algie, it's not that bad," Hollis said.

"That's 'cause *you* d-didn't barf."

Hollis sighed. "I still don't know what all that yellow stuff was that you threw up."

"Orange j-juice," Algie grumbled.

Leta smacked herself in the head. "Juice! That's why you didn't keel over!"

"I drank lots. It k-kept me from gettin' hungry."

A stewardess appeared and leaned over their seats.

"Are your seat belts fastened?" she asked.

"Is the b-bouncin' g-gonna start again?" Algie shot back, glaring at her.

She reached into the pocket on the back of the seat and pulled out a small bag. "If you feel sick this time, use this."

"I t-t-told you. *That's* not gonna help," Algie said, his expression growing more threatening. "D-don't you have a b-bowl?" He glanced at the bag. "A b-big bowl?"

Leta took the bag from the woman. "I'll take care of him. Sorry about the mess."

With an uncertain look, the woman moved on to the next set of seats.

Miss Violet turned around from the row in front of them. "He okay?"

Leta nodded. "He's still mad about the plane."

"Algie," Miss Violet said, "if CNN hadn't gotten these seats, we'd have had to go by bus. It would have taken a whole day to get to your grandmother instead of three hours."

Algie sucked on his bottom lip. "Planes are okay," he said at last.

Miss Violet turned back around, and Hollis and Leta sighed.

Hollis and Leta staggered together down the skyway and hung onto Algie, who kept trying to wriggle from their grasp. Miss Violet followed.

"Stop, Algie," Hollis said in a hoarse whisper as he struggled to hold on to the squirming boy. "I told you, there's no reason to run. The car will wait for us, and we won't see Gee until it takes us to the hospital."

"But Jonas's gonna be here! I wanna see him!"

"But we don't know if he's even here yet."

"He's here! I see him! Jonas!" Algie wriggled even harder. "He's over there!" He broke loose just as they reached the waiting area, and he ran across the room with Gnomie in his arms to be enveloped in the arms of his oldest brother.

Jonas straightened as the others approached. Algie, refusing to let go, changed his hold from around Jonas's neck to around his waist.

"Hollis!" Algie crowed. "Jonas lost his braids."

Jonas smiled and rubbed his short hair. "They got in my way."

Leta joined Algie in the hug, but Hollis hung back, glaring at his older brother.

"No hug, Blues?" Jonas asked. "I missed *you*."

"I guess I got in your way, too," Hollis said.

Jonas frowned. "I wouldn't say that."

"You tricked me. I felt like an idiot when I got back to the roof and you weren't with me."

"You know where I went. I figured you'd be glad I took care of it."

"I wanted to help. Why couldn't you have let me help?"

"I promised Gee I'd bring you straight back. I lived up to that promise. I didn't promise I'd come back right away. So I figured I could go get it done and be right back."

"You didn't come back at all! Gee got sick. We didn't know what to do."

"Sorry—it wasn't on purpose. She didn't have her medicine?"

Leta shook her head.

"I thought she always had it in her pocket. Listen, Hollis, I didn't know. And when I got the baby out, it was sick. You had it right. Too hot for him in that attic. Too hot for all of them. They had a blow-up swimmin' pool so we pulled it out and pumped it up, and then we floated down the street to the Claiborne bridge. There were cops there who took the family, but when I tried to go back to y'all, they wouldn't let me. They had to cuff me, I was fightin' so hard. I ended up at the airport with the family and the baby."

"Why'd they send you to the airport?" asked Leta. "Shouldn't they have taken them to the hospital?"

"They did. The airport *was* the hospital. They flew the family out to a hospital in North Dakota, and I helped take care of patients comin' into the airport for a couple days and then got put on a bus to the Astrodome. That's where I was when I saw you on CNN. You should have been there, Hollis. When Algie hit that guy, everyone in the TV room went crazy."

"I *was* there," Hollis said. "*Really* there. It was embarrassing. That Hathaway guy's nice, though."

"I know. He's the one who got me out here. Need to thank him when I see him. But Hollis, it was still funny. And everyone in that room needed a laugh. And I probably wouldn't have seen it at all if it hadn't been funny. I was only in there because the whole stadium was talkin' about it. They were playin' it every five minutes. Algie's famous in Texas."

Algie grinned.

"Besides," Jonas continued, "you two got Gee to a hospital somehow. Seems like you did a pretty good job. Anyone got the latest on how she's doin'?"

Hollis shook his head and at last joined the other three in their hug.

Once they found the car to take them to the hospital, Miss Violet knelt in front of the kids to see them at eye level. "Goodbye, Algie. Someday I want you to try tuna noodle casserole, and when you do, think of me."

Algie's scowl at the mention of tuna noodle casserole faded into a grin. He threw his arm around her neck.

"And Gnomie, take care of Algie for me."

Algie bobbed the figure forward and back, as though it were nodding.

"Leta," she said, "you keep studying that geography. I expect big things."

Leta nodded and hugged her.

"And Hollis. You keep working on those leadership skills and brilliant ideas, and you'll go far."

Hollis hugged her while enjoying Jonas's flabbergasted expression.

They all watched as Miss Violet disappeared down the flyway, on her way back to Charleston.

"Brilliant ideas, Blues? You holdin' out on me?"

Hollis shook his head.

"And at *some* point, someone's gonna have to tell me how Algie got his very own attack vampire garden gnome."

Hollis laughed. "I'll let Algie tell you about that."

The elevator stopped on the seventh floor of the hospital. Hollis, Jonas, Leta, and Algie exited next to the nurse's station. A nurse, holding a phone to her ear, glanced at them as they stepped out of the elevator. Hollis spied Miz Jackson sitting in a wheelchair next to the nurse and waved. Instead of waving back, she pointed at him.

"That's them!"

The nurse slammed down the phone and hurried toward them.

"You the people with the news crew?" asked the nurse, whose name tag said "Joyce."

As Hollis opened his mouth to deny knowledge of any news crew, Harry Hathaway emerged from a waiting room, spotted Hollis, and waved.

Chapter 27

The Vote

"You can't take a news crew into ICU," Joyce said to Jonas as she folded her arms and turned her back on Harry Hathaway.

"We aren't trying to break any rules," Mr. Hathaway began, but Hollis broke in.

"Is my grandmother okay?"

All eyes flew to the nurse. She put her hand on Hollis's shoulder and escorted him and his siblings down the hall to an office, leaving Harry Hathaway and his crew behind. She swung open the door, and Hollis saw a man sitting there. "Dr. Paine? The Williams children are here."

The doctor stood as Joyce and the children crowded into the office. "Well, I know how worried you are about your grandmother. But there's some good news."

Leta gave a tiny squeak of excitement at the words.

"Your grandmother had a small stroke when she first got here. We had to induce a coma while we made sure she was going to be okay. Yesterday evening, we brought her out of it. Her condition is still guarded, but she seems to be healing very well."

"So she's okay?" Hollis asked, bewildered.

"Basically, yes. She's being moved into a private room right now. When she's settled, you can see her."

Hollis, his brothers, and his sister broke into a noisy celebration.

Joyce waited for them to quiet down, then escorted them back down to the ICU. "Sit down and relax," she said. "We'll get you in as soon as we can."

The four children gathered outside Gee's room, the three youngest waiting for the oldest to open the door. Jonas caught Hollis's eye and gulped. "Wanna go in first, Blues?"

Hollis gave him a look of surprise.

"She might still be mad at me," Jonas explained.

Hollis grinned and opened the door.

Gee held out her arms, and all four children disappeared into a mass hug.

"Oh, Gee," Leta said in a muffled voice. "We were so scared. When those policemen came and you didn't wake up, we thought—we thought—"

Gee hushed her, pulling her into a tighter embrace. "I don't remember nothin' past Tuesday. It's all a blank until I woke up here. Tell me! Where on Earth have y'all been?"

Before anyone could answer, the door opened and a nurse entered with a tray. "Hi, Gee, we wondered if you wanted something to eat. Your doctor said you could have some soup."

Gee flopped her hand. "I'm not hungry now."

Algie hopped up from a chair. "W-what kind is it?" he asked.

"Algie hasn't been eating," Hollis said to Gee. "For a long time."

The nurse smiled at Algie. "Chicken noodle."

Hollis watched a grin take over Algie's face.

"Can he have it?" Hollis asked.

The nurse told Algie to sit, and then she placed the food on a rolling table and slid it in front of the little boy. Algie picked up the spoon and dug in.

"Now," Gee said, after the nurse had left the room, "who goes first?"

Leta told the story of what happened to the three youngest members of the family after Gee had left in the boat. Both Gee and Jonas exclaimed aloud when they heard about the house falling out from under the children's feet.

As Leta completed her story, Gee's voice lashed out, "Algie! Did you really not eat?"

"Y-yup!" Algie said through a mouthful of crackers.

Gee shook her head. "Stubborn! So Hollis, how'd you like bein' in charge?"

Hollis snorted. "It sucked."

"Thought it would." Gee said, smiling. "Okay, Jonas. Let's hear it."

Jonas's head dropped. "Sorry, Gee."

Gee nodded. "Should be. Go on."

Taking a deep breath, Jonas launched into his story. Hollis watched Gee's eyes soften as Jonas described the people he helped. For once, he was not jealous of Gee being proud of Jonas.

At the end of his tale, Jonas asked, "So where we gonna live, Gee? We goin' back to New Orleans?"

"One disaster at a time, Jonas," Gee said. "Thank God we all survived and are back together at last."

"Erm," Hollis said.

Everyone turned to him.

"We aren't *all* back together," he began, but he was interrupted by the door opening.

Harry Hathaway stuck his head into the room. "Mind if we come in and film a bit of the reunion?"

All four children started talking at once, trying to tell Gee about Harry Hathaway. Gee held up her hand and glared at the silver-haired man.

"You ain't one of them weather idiots, are ya?"

Harry Hathaway shook Gee's hand. "Thanks, ma'am. We appreciate the story."

"After what my grandson put you through, it was the least I could do." She sent an exasperated glance toward Algie, who hugged Gnomie and grinned.

Harry Hathaway herded his crew out of the room.

"Hollis," Gee said. "Tell me. What did you mean, 'we aren't all back together'?"

Hollis took a deep breath. "I meant Dad."

Jonas groaned. "Blues, you haven't changed a bit."

"I have, too. I know he might be dead or in jail. I know he might be a drug addict or a thief. But I don't think he left because of you or Mama. I know he only cares about himself. I just wanna see if he's alive so I can meet him. I'm—I'm curious."

"So you're sayin'," Gee said, "you'll be okay even if he's still the no-good, low-down piece of scum he was when he left your mama?"

Hollis grinned, and Gee eyed him in astonishment. "He probably is. And I can handle that, too. You know, Gee, you can't kick someone out of your family just because they're a jerk."

Gee snorted. "Very good, Hollis. As for me, I personally think you can, but I'd like to hear from the rest of you. Jonas?"

Hollis scrunched up his eyes.

"Don't worry, Blues. Been thinkin'. Wanna find him. I wanna tell him all about himself, but I'll wait to meet him first. Guess I'm curious, too."

Leta raised her hand. "I vote 'yes.' I want to know if he's alive."

Gee nodded at Algie, who had fallen asleep against Gnomie. "What about him?"

"Algie," Leta said, shaking him. "Wake up."

Algie sat up, blinking at everyone. "W-what?"

"Do you want to find Dad?" Leta asked.

Algie shrugged. "Is he l-lost?"

Hollis nodded. "He's lost from us."

"I just w-wanted to find Gee," Algie said. "But I g-guess we can find him, too." He settled back down in the chair, rested his cheek on Gnomie's belly, and went back to sleep.

"He didn't sleep well at the shelter, either," Leta told Gee. "Nightmares."

Gee nodded, rubbing the hairs on her chin. "He'll be okay. He's eatin' and sleepin' again already." She sighed. "Well children, I recently realized I may not live forever. I agree we need to find out if your jerk of a father is still alive. Easy to start. Call his mother in Baton Rouge."

Her eyes flew to Hollis. "You really think you can deal with whatever he comes with?"

Hollis grinned. "After this? I think I can deal with anything."

Gee choked on a laugh. "Let's get to it, then."

She told him the number. His hands shook as he punched it in. After two rings, someone picked up.

"Hello?"

"Grammy Williams?" he asked. "It's Hollis."

"Oh, Hollis—I just saw you all on CNN. Algie hittin' that man like that on national TV. I hope Gee's able to teach him better manners. Anyway, I'm relieved y'all are all right. Tell Gee thank you for calling so soon. This whole thing must have upset her terribly. It's not like her to be so thoughtful."

Hollis ignored the insult. "Grammy Williams, where is Dad?"

"Who?" Suspicion entered her voice. "Hollis? Does Gee even know you're on the phone?"

"Yes, Grammy. She's right here."

"Is she . . . *all* there? Nothin's happened to her brain or anythin', has it?"

"She's fine. Here." He handed Gee the phone.

"Hello, Sally. Nice talkin' to you, too." Gee rolled her eyes. "No, I'm fine. No, no head injuries. The children are worried. Do you know where he is?" As she listened, a doubtful expression began in her eyes, then spread all over her face. Hollis held his breath.

If he's dead, I don't know what I'll do.

Gee took the receiver from her ear. "He's there. Sally's gone to get him. Who wants to talk first?"

All eyes turned to Hollis, who glanced around hopefully. "Me?"

Even Gee laughed at that one. "Who else?" Jonas asked.

Hollis held the phone up to his ear, waiting.

A deep voice sounded. "Hello?"

Hollis took a deep breath. "Dad?"